PTBT

For Roxana Josephine... my little girl.

Acknowledgments:

I'd like to thank Laura for her beautiful heart and unwavering friendship. She is my soul mate and my confidant. Without her support and brilliant work as my editor I would be hiding in a corner somewhere. Thank you to Dustin for being super talented with computers and design. I am so thankful to have worked with a professional with such a great sense of humor and genuine care and also for appreciating my thorough and detailed ways. Thank you to my brother Ryan for advice, insight and support. Thank you to Ellie who randomly and continually comes into my life with little bits of genius! To my uncles Craig and Aaron who believed enough in me to throw some cash my way so that I could get my book published and create my business, your faith is felt in my bones. To Erin for being my sounding board, my love, my biggest fan. Our conversations are the cornerstones of growth, movement and change. Imagining what I would do without you makes me gag and puke in my mouth so let's just skip it. To my mom Cheryl, dad Bruce and second mom Michele, thank you for the openness, love, support and encouragement through my whole experience with Roxana and the development of my PTBT Method as well as the writing of this book. I feel hugely fortunate to have you all as my foundation. To Alex for trusting me with our daughter, to giving me the OK to experiment with the unknown and to catching up on child support so that I had an extra few months to survive while I wrote this book! You are undoubtedly needed and valued. Thank you to my many friends and family members who were accepting of my choices and excited about the truth I was discovering. To the friends and family members who completely ignored what I was doing and kept your scoffing to a minimum, you are appreciated as well! Thank you to Calypso for the deep love, respect and friendship you consistently give me. Your positive, vibrant energy is always welcome. To Maranhoa for seeing me, loving me and making it your mission to break the thin glass wall I was trying to build around my heart. Your gentle, nurturing and very firm wisdom is music to my ears and a feast for my soul. Thank you to Michael for everything you have shown me. Finally, thank you to the Universe for listening to me and offering me the opportunity to trust myself and to recognize my intuition. Thanks for pushing me around and scaring the shit out of me, thanks for making me cry and hurt and question. Without the depth of despair and fear how would I know when I was truly feeling the height of joy and courage?

Table of Contents

A New Path...

My name is Angela Graham; I am a 31 year old single mother of an incredibly smart and beautiful little girl named Roxana Josephine. We live in the lush, wet, emerald green city of Seattle. This book that I have written, to the sounds of pattering rain and brilliant everlasting color, is the love child of a tremendous journey we took together. I was introduced to an idea while pregnant for the first time, which was foreign to me and

the opposite of everything I'd been taught about babies. I applied its basic principles to the relationship I held with my newborn and I was forever changed. The connection we created, the seemingly impossible feats Roxana easily maneuvered and the utterly surprising awareness that my daughter projected then and still carries, has been an inspiration for many.

The idea I was so eagerly drawn to is widely known as "Infant Potty Training" as well as such beautiful descriptions as "Elimination Communication" and "Natural Infant Hygiene." Both are wonderful names and a more gentle way to explain this amazing natural phenomenon. I have chosen to refer to this action and awareness with infants as the *"PTBT Method"* or simply "PTBT" throughout my book. PTBT Method was created with, "wisdom from the past to better our future" as the foundation. PTBT stands for *Potty Trained By Two* and refers to a baby's innate ability to recognize his/her elimination needs, the baby's desire to release in an upright position and away from the body as well as his/her ability to communicate those needs from birth. It is the belief that if it were up to an infant, all potty training would be accomplished well before 2 years of age.

"Method" stands for obtaining practical knowledge and making the choice to assist infants in their biological journey. This ability is in every healthy infant around the world but they cannot accomplish their elimination needs without the assistance of aware parents and caretakers. Exactly like eating, sleeping and cuddling, babies need someone else to help them in their endeavors. My PTBT Method accepts an infant's instinct and knowledge as fact and guides a parent through the means of accomplishing safe, educated, healthy and happy potty training before 2 years old.

The act itself is as old as the first reproducing human beings. For many thousands of years and in many cultures around the world there was no name for the way parents naturally trusted their infants' abilities and worked with their elimination needs. In our current culture everything is named, categorized, labeled and dissected. I wanted my title to very proudly carry the words, "potty trained" as I fully believe that in our society's near future we will find children's sections in popular stores entitled, "potty training" and "diaper training". There will no longer be a need to differentiate *when* parents start potty training their children, it will simply be whether they choose to teach them how to eliminate in a toilet or how to eliminate in a diaper. Eventually, the diaper sections will dissolve and end up being one expensive and very short aspect of our history.

My book serves as a catalyst for this change! What I have written is not the beginning and end all of what there is to know. It is not the best researched or most scientific approach. I am not a medical doctor and I do not have a PhD in psychology. I am not wealthy, I am not a hippy, or religious, or anti-society, or extreme or even married with a supportive husband. I am a very real, diverse, single woman who found so much joy and inspiration in the presence of the tiny human being that I had put forth such extreme physical effort to produce!

I found transformation in this ancient and carnal knowledge. My story is a true, authentic tale of a first time mother living in a very modern and advanced society. It is a story of tough relationships, stress, financial insecurity, change and pushing the boundaries of comfort. It's a story of deeply rooted questions and smoothly hidden answers, of utter joy, surprise, power and most importantly, awareness. I am a genuine woman who struggled in our current dwindling economy and pushed through an exhausting and painful relationship. A woman who tried something a bit different and found a brand new world of trust and capability! I was able to do what I did with Roxana without flipping my life upside down, without so many variables and we succeeded!

This is why I write this book to you. If my daughter and I can climb to the great heights that we did, then *anyone* can. We experienced such amazing success with our very own version of infant potty training, our PTBT Method, that I felt it was a duty of mine to share our story. I want to let parents know that our children deserve to be listened to; they deserve to be taught that their communication is important and is heard. They deserve to learn as early as possible that their bodies communicate to them and that it is vital that they listen and be able to interpret their own needs.

This concept is a large part of my love of PTBT Method, I definitely believe we tend (especially in our modern society) to isolate ourselves from ourselves. We hide our feelings, emotions, fears and joys; we downplay our instincts and awareness of ourselves and others. We are not taught to pay attention to our true desires, we are taught to desire what is given to us in our environments. We are taught to desire what is external and not internal. I believe allowing our babies to discover their body's abilities and their intuition we are giving them a head start in the very best direction. They will take this experience and repeat it over and over again. Imagine people paying attention to their true needs and communicating those with the people around them without fear of exclusion! What a wonderful idea and way to live.

The purpose of PTBT Method is to create accessibility for all parents, living in the many diverse phases of modern family dynamics. The major reasons for this approach are to save time and keep it simple. I tried to read my first infant potty training book a couple of weeks after Roxana was born but it was long and overwhelming, I ended up skimming my way through it. I wanted to write a book that could be read through, understood and implemented with ease. My goal is to teach the families and caretakers who feel they don't have the time or patience for such a practice.

My book is about moderation, it is for people who are interested in infant potty training but have no idea how to really make it happen. It is for people who can't imagine giving their babies diaper free time or at least as much of it as is required by other teachings. It is for the aware parent who wants to be earth friendly, wants to save some money and has a desire to connect with their kids. Many people are busy and bustling and aren't sure how to accomplish infant potty training without creating a total upheaval in their day to day lives.

Potty Trained By Two is meant to bridge the gap between those folks who blast through disposables without a second glance and the few who have time to stay home with their naked infants' day in and day out. Don't misunderstand me, there is nothing wrong with the way anyone lives their life and the way anyone parents. My book is not about making people feel guilty or like "tools" because they have always used diapers or never have. I want people to know there is a common ground; you don't have to be so extreme on either end. We all do the very best that we can with the knowledge we have. My hope is to offer enough knowledge that it might make many lives, of parents and children alike, more comfortable and filled with the happiness my daughter and I share.

The PTBT Method offers techniques that when used, will generate quick, positive change. This book will guide you *briefly* through the history of this infant phenomenon, potty training around the globe, scientific realities and conspiracy. The psychology of bodily awareness, a smattering of thought provoking concepts, our personal story and an easy to follow step by step program that anyone can participate in!

Our technique veered off naturally from what most of the books suggest. It is a method that will improve your communication with your infant/child, will encourage them to understand and pay attention to their own bodies and functions, it will foster and develop an environment in which parent and child can practice positive feedback. PTBT Method is meant to lead families through responsibility, awareness, communication and personal achievement.

PTBT Method can be accomplished without too much struggle and strife. It is an attainable goal even given the smallest of effort, so welcome to this new path. I hope you enjoy it as much as I did! I hope you have your mind blown and your thoughts changed. I hope your child blossoms from recognition and the bond you generate together feels stronger than you ever imagined. Enjoy.

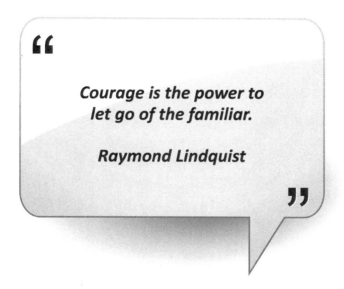

"

Courage is the power to let go of the familiar.

Raymond Lindquist

"

Our Adventure Begins…

0 to 3 months:

In all of my years teaching in schools, assisting in daycare centers, babysitting and working as a nanny I had never heard of PTBT or anything even remotely like it. It had never occurred to me that the diaper was something highly overrated and that we might not need it. If I'd ever questioned or even thought about diapers it was to determine whether I'd use disposable or cloth, whether to get a diaper service or not. I had never questioned their total and complete infiltration into parenting and the life of infants. Disposable diapers

just seemed so convenient and such a natural part of an infant's life and an accepted part of being a parent.

I first heard of PTBT when I was approximately 8 months pregnant. I was in a birthing class, when a young couple who had just given birth for the first time, shared their story. The new mother was glowing from her amazing natural birth and mentioned how her and her husband had begun "cueing" their son at about 2 weeks to pee and poop and that he'd been responding. I immediately asked a billion questions because I was totally blown away. My mind screamed, "What are you even talking about?!!"

They had begun making a pssst sound while the infant eliminated and at other times to stimulate and simulate release for their infant; they had not used diapers and instead used a little cloth for spills. I was shocked and very intrigued. Their explanations and the science behind cueing sounded completely legitimate and I, for the first time in my life, had the disposable diaper vale lifted from my eyes!

My mind started to wander and to fantasize about what people did for thousands and thousands of years without diapers. I imagined parents from all over the world in millions of different living arrangements, certain that parents were practicing smarter and quicker ways of dealing with infant excrement. I did not see them keeping their kids in diapers until 3 and 4 years old or higher like we do in our society. Imagine the amount of extra work that would be for parents who were outside in fields, working farms, on the move, packing their homes on their backs or resettling monthly. Surely not!

Then I thought about people wagon training across the United States and that they wouldn't have been able to afford the nuisance of diapers filled with poop along their trek. They would have had to come up with a more efficient and hygienic way to release waste than into a sack that they would have to carry around with them. I realized that diapers generate a major problem when you have nowhere to wash them. It only made sense that one of the first things you would do as a new parent would be to focus on your infant's most basic needs and functions which are hunger, sleep and elimination. The mother takes care of hunger by carrying this essential complex right in her sweet breasts. Sleep is vital and the creation of a safe, warm sleeping environment was required and paid attention to. Human excrement was a constant reality and working effectively with infant elimination and waste disposal was a necessity just as it was for every other human in the family.

I asked a few more questions and it turned out another couple, who were due with their second child, the week before me, were experienced with PTBT. They had been very successful potty training their first son, who was finished at 15 months and they were wholeheartedly planning on practicing this awareness again with their second child. I asked about books they'd read, but at the time I was expecting my first baby and was reading about 10 books on birthing and what to do after so I didn't end up getting any of the books until after Roxana was born.

My awareness had changed and although my intrigue was great, I was preoccupied. By the time I was ready I had forgotten the name of the books. One day when Roxana was about 2 weeks old I decided to try out the small town library down the hill. I went up to the information counter and asked if they had any books on infant potty training. The librarian said,

"Oh, yes. Over here!"

She wore a broad smile on her face as she escorted me to the potty training section. She then proceeded to point out several books on basic diaper based training for children 2, 3 and 4. When I asked again and clarified what I was looking for the woman gave me a cockeyed look and tilted her head like something was draining out her ear. She stared wide eyed at little, tiny Roxana, a small warm bundle wrapped on my chest. When she finished emptying her ear onto the carpet, we went back to the computer and did a search. It turned out she had a book called *Infant Potty Training* by Laurie Boucke.

I thanked her profusely for her help and checked out the book they had on PTBT. Somehow I had a feeling this would not be the first time I would come across someone who looked at me like I was off my nut! I read what I had time for but mostly skimmed through as the book was long and

well... I was a new mom with lots of new duties! I felt I had the gist of it down, I mainly needed to pay attention, believe in both our abilities and try something new (or in reality, very old, as it had been used for eons before disposables were introduced!) Roxana and I began our version of PTBT when she was 3 weeks old.

I began by sitting her back up against my thighs with my knees bent and feet flat on the ground when she would poop. This was not intentional;

initially I didn't know what she was doing except squirming around. One day, she was worming around so much that I sat her up in my lap to get a look at her so I could figure out what the heck was going on. I realized then that she had to poop, her forehead would get red and she would really work on it. She was the cutest pooper I have ever seen. Like a crazy little old man, bearing down with this furrowed brow. I guess part of the extreme cuteness was that she was so tiny and that she was born early so all her hair wasn't in. She had this Franciscan monk hairdo, where the front and top were mostly fuzz and she sported a ring of thick hair around the circumference of her head, like a little bald halo.

Roxana seemed so relieved to be sitting in an upright position, leaning comfortably flush against my legs and looking at me, that we started getting into this habit and it never left us. By the time she was a month old she didn't poop lying down anymore. After doing this action for a few weeks I was amazed at how well she'd communicate her needs to me. I started questioning whether it was really happening or not as I had a difficult time believing that an infant could communicate on that level. I had never been told that they could so I just assumed she was not aware.

I was very, *very* wrong and so thrilled to learn through the whole course of this experience just how brilliant and capable our infants are! So, in my state of doubt, I would test her for evidence. I began ignoring her signs for periods of time instead of immediately lifting her up for her poop. I would just lay there next to her, letting her squirm around to see if she really was communicating or if I had just been lucky or imagining things. She indeed was communicating!

I never let her worm around for too long but long enough that when I'd finally pick her up and put her against my knees she'd look at me with this exasperated expression,

"MOM! What is *wrong* with you, can't you see I have to poop, *now*!?"

She would, very seriously, let out a long, loud sigh as if she were annoyed with me and also from pure relief. *Every single time* I tested her this way she'd poop almost as soon as she was upright and after she scolded me, of course. After testing her, a handful of times, I realized I had my scientific, factual evidence and I no longer needed to torture her. We were really doing it so I went back to responding naturally to her needs.

I had learned when I skimmed through the potty training book, that creating a verbal cue is a necessary part of working with infants on elimination. The sound you create and make during their physical release will sync up with their brain so that once it is established after several sessions, a parent can potentially make the cue noise when the infant doesn't necessarily initiate it and the baby will pee or poop... on cue. I was fascinated by this idea and began trying it out as soon as I read about it.

I was sitting Roxana up to poop and I didn't really know when she peed so I just decided to use a pssst sound while she released. I also would softly grunt and moan a bit when she was really working on a poop. I would take deep breaths and sigh them out. Roxana would look at me and copy my sounds. This made her feel secure and supported while working so hard. I started talking to her about it and telling her everything that was going on.

"Hey, you're pooping sitting up! Great job, sweetie!"

I'd talk to her every time so her experience was validated. I started signing to her also, showing her the sign for poop while she released and while I spoke the word to her. When she finished I always praised her and we moved right along with our day.

In the books that I read, an observation day was mentioned as a great way to determine your infant's elimination schedule. I was interested in learning how to let her poop outside of her diaper so I thought I'd give it a go. 5 weeks after Roxana's birth I tried an observation day; it turned out to be rather interesting...

I chose to sit on the couch breastfeeding Roxana with her diaper off and a little waterproof pad on my lap. I had wipes ready and my little notebook. She pooped the first time and I jotted it down then stopped to clean up. Once I sat back down with a fresh pad she pooped again and then again and then again. According to my notes she pooped 8 times within a 45 minute period. I had a pad full of poop and when I went to lift her up to wipe her and get off the couch she projectile vomited on my face and into my hair!

I struggled to get up without destroying my couch and floor forever and shuffled to the kitchen where I had her little bath basin on the counter next to the sink. I was not wearing anything but panties as was my normal ensemble in the very beginning. It was either spend the day topless or spend the day in a perpetual wet t-shirt contest, which I would have won given the beautiful expansion of my breasts! On a quick note, women who choose *not* to breastfeed for reasons like ego, embarrassment, and perfection obsessions; I would like to point out that your breasts will change from giving birth and breastfeeding your baby, everyone experiences this. Our society tends to focus on the negative aspects or possibilities. I would like to tell you that for the 2 ½ years I breastfed my daughter I had an incredibly luscious, yummy rack that even I couldn't keep my eyes off of! Being a woman born with small breasts it was really fun vamping around with some curvy knockers for awhile, sans the surgery and fake application, they were as real as it gets!

I started to mop up Roxana and my hair with a warm, wet cloth and we both got covered in water. Next I put the basin in one side of the sink to fill it up for a nice bath and I felt a hot sensation running down the length of my body from my chest to my toes. Roxana was peeing on me. So there I was in my sunny kitchen, virtually naked with puke in my hair, breast milk leaking from my nipples, hot urine on my body and a pad full of poop in the sink! All I could do at that point was laugh! Needless to say I did *not* partake in another observation day.

Little Bits of
Encouragement

Remember you have the ability to start fresh every day.

The day was a fluke, I knew Roxana regularly pooped first thing in the morning and then it varied throughout the day, but often times she would only poop the one time, right in the morning. I felt too overwhelmed to figure it all out without her diapers on, at that point. We got into our routine throughout the day and she sat upright to poop without fail. Even at night, sometimes she'd wake me up with her squirm and once she was in position, she'd relieve herself and we'd go back to sleep.

Roxana was a pretty small baby 6 pounds, 1 oz at birth and just had a slim, petite figure so I was concerned about her disappearing on the potty chair when I was ready to transition her. I was also concerned about her getting cold sitting on the plastic and marks or indentations on her butt causing her potential pain or discomfort. My remedy to this was creating soft and comfortable padding for the potty chair. Something that would make the chair feel more secure and warm. Initially, I began using a receiving blanket folded on the back and two cloth diapers folded up on the seated area. This worked fine but was often a pain for me trying to keep the diapers folded and not sliding into the feces and urine! I eventually developed a knack for it but it was difficult for everyone else who happened to assist Roxana on her potty, I knew I had to create something more fitting so there were no factors getting in the way of her natural elimination.

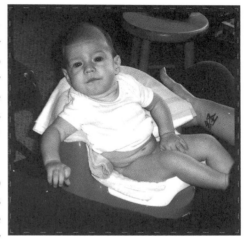

The design I came up with and have to offer now is wonderful! What I wouldn't give to have had the idea and ability to have had the idea and ability to create it back then! My padding is specifically designed to fit the Baby Bjorn potty chair *with the back* as I believe this adds an element of safety and relaxation that the other potty chairs don't. Also you will only buy one chair and it will be perfect for the whole length of your child's elimination journey. I call the padding, the *Sweet Seat* and it adds depth and comfort to the back of the chair and to the seat so small babies will feel more at ease.

I transferred Roxana to the potty chair at 3 months. I positioned the chair in between my legs and had her facing me like she was already used to; I did everything exactly the same but removed her diaper. I remember being nervous that she wouldn't like it but she was thrilled, in fact she much preferred it. She realized with this new addition to our routine that no more "mess" got on her; she didn't have to feel sticky and stinky and go through the extensive wiping up process. I believe by maintaining the same comfortable position she was used to and maintaining our connection and eye contact with me she felt quite safe and secure trying something new. I always used her supportive, warm padding so she didn't get chilled by the plastic and so the potty fit her better.

4 to 6 months:

When Roxana was born I was living with her father. We loved each other very much but had not planned my pregnancy and neither of us had previous children so we did not know *really* what to expect. Our first attempt at living together had been stressful as well because we built a cabin together virtually by ourselves and lived in it through a very cold, snowy winter without accoutrements like running water, a bathroom, insulation or a finished floor. We hoped that the second time around things wouldn't be so difficult; but with a baby on the way it looked like we started off with a bang!

We tried to create the most supportive environment as possible for our new child by staying together but it was strained as we did things *very* differently. We lived in a wonderful three bedroom house with amazing views of the Strait of Juan de Fuca on one side and the Olympic mountain range on the other. Roxana's father had traded our rent for a year with his friend who owned the house, for a little stock in the property our cabin was on. We had a garden, a big yard and a huge garage. I was in charge of keeping everything clean, doing laundry, shopping for food and other needs, caring for Roxana, tending the garden and lawn and making meals. I was utterly exhausted and had points where I felt I was splitting into thousands of pieces from the amount I was giving out.

He wasn't ready to be responsible, to have a relationship, a house, garden and a baby all at once. He didn't know what to do so he didn't do anything. This is common for so many dads who have children unexpectedly but they must realize that the mothers don't have the luxury of a *choice*. We cannot just hide out or be selfish with our time. Having a baby is an extraordinary opportunity to grow and develop true strength, unfortunately the stresses tend to scare people off and we all end up with shattered hearts and families.

When you have a little life that is so dependent on you it takes everything. It is exhausting and difficult and every mother should be given tremendous praise and love for their sacrifices. As trying as it can be, it is by far, the most important job one can do. I learned that there were distinct reasons for the need of two parents, a mother cannot truly nurture the way she needs to if the father does not help her. It is his job to give to her so that she may give to the child. This is crucial in the very beginning especially as it takes some time getting used to being so utterly needed by an infant!

There were times of tremendous joy and solidarity, of love and affection. Her father helped with household duties, lawn care and cooking, but it was touch and go. My partner was not working and when he did it was marginal. Rent was covered but all other bills and needs were barely met. I paid off his debts and mine with my credit card, bought a car and everything we needed with my credit also. I was staying home with my baby but I was also living off "imaginary money" and I started receiving state assistance for the first time in my life, a big ego blow for me.

Through the state assistance program I received food stamps, medical care and varying other additions. They had a wonderful birthing support group with counselors and lactation consultants to guide you through any difficulties. There were group meetings available for all and many families would come in from all walks of life, as Roxana was born in the wave of a crashing economy. I only attended a couple of meetings but I was asked to come back and teach PTBT to the group. I was thrilled to share my findings with everyone and to encourage the new parents to "check in" with their infants.

Roxana and I had been doing so well with our PTBT Method but we were still in the early stages at 4 months old. I wasn't sure if our cue was fully established and if it would "work" when I gave an official demonstration. After discussing the history and theories with the class I showed them the mechanics of how to sit and communicate and then I put Roxana on the potty chair and made the pssst sound. Everyone watched me like I was completely out of my mind! They had never heard of anything like this, just as I hadn't, but I tend to be very open minded, whereas some people are uncomfortable with ideas they aren't familiar with. I made the cue for about a minute when all of the sudden she started to pee. I was thrilled, every single person gasped and their eyes went huge! Roxana was mellow and relaxed and looked at us like, "What's the big deal, yo? I'm just peeing like I always do."

The entire group and all of the staff were so amazed that they didn't believe their ears; I had to pass the potty bowl around so everyone could peer in and see the pee for themselves! It was a riot! So many questions came pouring in and many were inspired to try it out right away. i want people to realize that anyone can accomplish this kind of communication and foster growth with their babies, regardless of the circumstances. It takes energy, attention and time but no more than diaper training your babies. It is a different method but it pays off in the most substantial ways and even if it seems like more effort in the beginning it surely comes out way ahead in the end.

Another aspect, besides cueing, that the group was intrigued by was using sign language. I am an enormous fan and after my experience with Roxana a huge proponent of teaching signs from birth. I have read about some sign language backlash that came out once the practice started to become popular for hearing babies. Some people were suggesting that parents not teach it to hearing babies because it would limit their ability to talk. The child would concentrate too much on signing and would, in effect, be slower at developing his/her verbal skills.

Ha! is all I have to say. My daughter is not quite 3 years old and she's been talking nearly two years now. Just before 2 she became very verbal and now she explains things to me in full paragraphs, even using words in the correct tense. Roxana asks alarmingly aware questions and shows a strong understanding of semantics. I think she developed this partly due to her experience with so many types of communication. She understands nearly everything and if she doesn't, she asks. Sign language use with infants and toddlers has become very popular in the last few years and with good reason. Developmentally it takes longer for children to learn how to speak than it does to show simple signs with their hands, they learn how to point and grasp and take things apart before they can master all of the nuances of a verbal language. I have read that some children begin signing as early as 6 months!

Usually it takes children until 2 years old to get a firm enough grasp on verbal language to communicate their needs and to ask questions, many children take much longer. I highly recommend using sign language for all kinds of words and actions, I chose to use signs for eating/nursing activities, potty words and a few others but I did not expand the vocabulary to include inanimate objects, games, letters and a number of other options. A lot of parents do and it is nothing but beneficial.

As far as PTBT Method is concerned I highly suggest you learn the signs for "potty", "good job", "all done", "help", "milk" and "more" to build your vocabulary. With these few simple signs you have your bases covered. You can create "home" signs, meaning that they are signs you came up with yourself but are not actually registered American Sign Language signs. This is fine to do; however, you need to make sure that all people involved in your child's care know your *specific "home"* signs, so as not to cause confusion. I would recommend knowing the ASL signs especially if you are only planning on doing a few, they are easy and there are books and instructional videos readily available to make sure you are doing them right.

Your baby may not respond to the signs for several months but just continue to show them consistently because your child is taking it all in. Sign language use is a very effective means to expand a child's awareness, communication and learning potential. Most importantly it is a means of minimizing confusion on the part of the caretaker, allowing for a more relaxed and happy child because her/his needs are met without too much complication and frustration. In my experience, all forms of communication and constant, *clear* communication are keys to a fully diverse and well developed child. Why deprive a child of a possibility to understand? Why deprive a child of anything that has to do with healthy development?

Roxana and I were practicing the verbal cueing, the physical positioning, using sign language and communicating exactly what was happening, as well as praise for the act. I definitively saw pride and a sense of accomplishment in her face, eyes, and expression. This was something she could feel, understand, and control. There aren't too many things at that age babies can feel in control of or that they are choosing to do themselves. I think, from observing Roxana, that even for infants, it is a great sensation to realize your own power to use your body and to understand your body. The mind connects with the physical and the holistic awareness begins.

We had just been winging it as far as potty training with no real schedule so I decided to set a goal for myself to keep our practice active and focused. I chose to try to catch Roxana's morning poop in the potty chair and that was it. I figured this would be the easiest as it was obvious when she had to go and with everything else going on at home it wouldn't take up too much time. Roxana peed nearly every time she would poop and sometimes would pee and skip the poop, either way I was getting something or everything each morning!

Now that we had transferred her to the potty, we were cueing, communicating and praising, and we had established a consistent morning practice, she responded amazingly well. We kept this routine going for awhile with not too many additional potty opportunities, however, it was very easy for me to see when she had to poop so I would put her on the potty during the day when she had to go. This worked great for me but was difficult for her dad or anyone else who happened to be spending some time with her to know when she had to go. I realized it was time to implement more of a pattern and started offering her more potty time.

I chose to go with the most logical time, right after she got up from sleeping. I started putting her on the potty after naps just as I would do in the morning. Every single time was a winner! I was saving a handful of diapers a day and several wipes not to mention the tubes of diaper rash ointment that went unopened for months (until I finally decided to open one and put it on her any way just so I could use some!). I would let Roxana have diaper free time directly after she went potty in her chair. This made perfect sense as she had just gone to the bathroom and the chances of her going again within the next half hour were pretty slim. She loved it.

We lived on the Olympic Peninsula when Roxana was born in the spring so by the time she was a few months old we were outside all the time. I would take her diaper off when we were laying around in the lawn enjoying the sun and the sweet smells of summer. I'd lay a blanket out, put a towel or a water proof little pad under her and I'd just let her go commando. She was overjoyed. Being that we had more of a schedule down I got into bringing her potty chair along with us for outings. We'd go to Lake Crescent, a phenomenally gorgeous deep lake with the most vivid blue and green colors. I would take her

swimming with her naked, wrapped to my body, with a long piece of soft cotton. I'd set up a picnic area with her potty chair right on the side. She'd be without a diaper the whole time and when I'd put her on the potty I'd position an umbrella behind it so she had a cool shaded spot she could relax in and release.

I'd also take her to the beach on the coast. My girlfriend Erin and her daughter came to visit when Roxana was around 5 months and we had a picnic at the beach. I had told Erin what I'd been doing but she had never seen it. She was amazed and her daughter Esme thought it was the coolest thing ever, seeing such a small baby on the potty! Esme bragged about her "little sister" to everyone. We brought the potty chair along and after lunch Roxana showed signs of needing to poop so up she went. Erin laughed like crazy because it really is so astounding to see. She witnessed Roxana's ease and

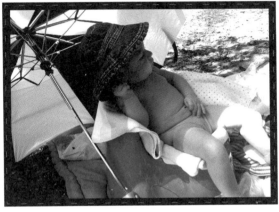

joy with this arrangement. Roxana did her business and I cleaned her up and took the bowl of the potty to a location where I dug a deep hole and buried her little poop. Just like going camping. I scrubbed the bowl out with sand and we were good to go. I really feel those days that Roxana got to spend outside with the sun and air on her body felt so good to her. Babies need this, as do all children, especially when they wear diapers.

Roxana and I also went on a walk everyday using our *Moby* wrap. I started bundling her in the wrap without her diaper after she had used the potty. It was so much more comfortable for her, not having the pinching or tightness around her belly from a diaper while curled up. I was nervous the first couple of times I tried this because the last thing I wanted on our beautiful walk was hot pee or even hotter poop covering us both and having to run back to the house a bumbling sticky mess! Well... it never happened.

Once I transferred Roxana to the potty chair (at 3 months old), she so loved and regularly eliminated into her potty that she did not poop in a diaper until just before she was 7 months! It was amazing! I know she would have gone longer but we were visiting friends in Boise and we both got sick. It was her first time to be sick in her life and very rare for me. On the second day of sickness she had a fever and blasted diarrhea into her diaper! The poor little thing, opened up her eyes really wide like she was just as surprised as I was that it came out. I laughed really hard and told her not to worry; that it was ok, she was sick and she had an accident. It was so freaking funny to see her innocent face projecting utter disbelief. I realized that she and I had come a long way with our practice! Roxana got over her illness and she went right back to pooping in her potty.

7 to 9 months:

By the time Roxana was 6 months old we had experienced several dry overnights and up to 17 hours of the same diaper use, (*completely* dry and clean). We were really connecting. Unfortunately, things were not so good with her dad and I and we split up. Roxana and I moved out just before our trip to Boise. I was so stressed and busy trying to move us by myself that I felt I couldn't maintain her additional potty times. I had to pack everything, her father would not help. I cleaned the garage and the house, put ads in the paper to rent it out, showed the home, got everything covered with new renters for his friend who owned the home. Had a huge yard sale, rented the truck and my mom came out to help me load. We did it together while also caring for Roxana. I was a virtual shell of a woman, not to mention that her dad hung around fighting with me but not lifting a finger to assist. It was awful, my utter exhaustion was definitely the reason my immune system was down and I had gotten sick on our trip.

I was amazed at Roxana's awareness while we moved from Port Angeles to Tacoma. I could only manage to put Roxana on the potty for her morning opportunity and at no other regular time for almost two months. I had too much going on to try at other points in the day. During this time she pooped every morning, there were zero accidents. I do not know if this was intentional or just random but that is what happened. Roxana and I had been on a pretty regular schedule and our practice was coming along beautifully when everything shifted. I was hurting so badly that I just didn't have the energy and I felt I needed to back off as well as being so busy packing up the house then unpacking our new one. The only diaper I changed that had poop in it for all of October and November was from her cold in Boise.

It was crazy, Roxana knew she always had the opportunity to use the potty in the morning and she took it. I believe she sensed and felt the changes and of course I explained to her what was happening. I told her I wouldn't be able to put her on the potty as much but I was stunned to see how she responded in such a silent and strong way. I know there were a few random times throughout those two months that Roxana made it obvious she had to go poop at other points during the day. When I saw those signs I would put her on the potty but I was not offering her our regular schedule. I was amazed by this and when we finally got settled into our apartment, my pain subsided and things mellowed out. She began pooping more often but still very regularly in the morning and I put her back on the schedule of opportunities.

It was an enormously stressful time for me having left her father and starting out completely on our own. We couldn't even talk to each other we were completely off one another's radar. I had changed so much; life didn't look the same to me. My *understanding* was biological so my changes came as a very natural and deeply intuitive process. Men don't have this luxury (as hard as it is ladies, I do believe it's a *gift*) they have to make the changes in themselves through observation, faith and indirect connection. It often takes longer for them to *get* the fundamental changes that take place when a baby is made and born. Women know it in their pores the minute another human begins to grow in their bodies and this awareness is cemented when a woman experiences the exaltation of birth. I was devastated from the way we had fallen apart and from his inability to connect with his role in our lives.

I felt so helpless and extremely depressed at points through the first couple of months. Besides the negativity from my relationship crashing I was also experiencing tremendous fear about finances. I had always been a very savvy woman and could come up with work when I needed it but this was a totally different situation. I had another life that was completely dependent on me. I did not have the flexibility I was used to. I had a very small amount of money left from my credit cards for rent and bills and I was receiving food stamps. I knew I could live simply enough to make our lives work with the money I had left from my credit but the major issue was paying my credit card bills. If I paid those off with the interest and rising payments there would be no way to make it on my own.

I faced a very tough decision for me, either I kept up with my credit cards and stayed in the good "zone" or I let them go, faced a dropping credit allowance and score and use my money to survive for a few precious months. I had busted my butt to establish very good credit and it would go down the tubes as fast as I could blink. I had worked really hard for such a long time and I felt weird to not be working outside of my house. This predicament was during the height of our economic crash and all I kept hearing about were billion dollar bailouts for the major corporate banks. I questioned why there wasn't a bailout to assist our economy from the most fundamental aspect of our society...the people. Why were we left to struggle, have our homes and cars taken away, and have our families torn apart due to the need of both parents to work full time to make ends meet? All the while major banks and corporations take precedence over the bread and butter of our society... *families*. There was a lot of worry and fear going on around that time for so many people. I began centering my thoughts and energy into my heart. When I funneled out all of the "expectations" and "desires" of our society it was very clear and easy for me to see what was more important.

I *truly* desired and innately *needed* to spend the first year of Roxana's life at home with her. My daughter and I both deserved to have that time together. We do not have a society that is set up to support women taking the truly appropriate amount of time with their babies, or parents in general, for that matter. The first year in a new human's life is such a transformative time, the *most important*, to set a new person's foundation. So many people suffer from a lack of intimacy and connection. That much needed time to explore each other, to foster trust and strengthen the bond that will keep you close for the rest of your life is vital in early development.

I figured there was all the time in the world to stress about money, years and years to work and save and scrimp. The only time that my little Roxana would be an infant and would *physically* need me so badly was for the first year of her life. When that is over it does not ever come back. I chose to have a baby, I chose to be a mother and then I chose to give us both the gift of intimacy through personal sacrifice. Once I found this space in my heart and I could feel the truth of my *mothering instincts* emanating in my blood I was content. I chose to completely avoid paying any of my debt and to only focus on the bills involved in our survival. I knew this was temporary and I knew with my whole being that it was right.

We can choose to make our lives better. It may seem like we can't but if I learned anything through this whole experience it is to trust my instincts and to act on what I know is right. Even if my instinct goes against absolutely everything our society tells me, even if it goes against logic and "the rules" and developing a safety net. People who really live their lives take risks. This truth is written over and over again throughout history and in every successful person's memoir. You *must* follow what is in your heart despite your fear and then you *will* succeed.

I made it through because I knew as hard as it was I still had many things to be thankful for. Also, if I was to fall apart, who would care for my daughter? That thought in itself has pushed me above and beyond. I know I could make it through anything to foster a secure life for her. I had chosen, after much stress and fretting to stay home with Roxana for the remainder of her first year. Despite occasional bouts of worry I trusted my instincts and both Roxana and I thrived. I started writing an outline for this book and wrote a children's book based on a lullaby I made up for Roxana. It was a tough time for people all over and I made the best of our situation with a comfortable, clean, safe environment that was very mellow and loving.

During this time of introversion and calm I was opened to a new element of PTBT Method. Trust your intuition! I remember reading about the ability to tap into your instincts to help guide you into intuitively knowing when your baby had to eliminate. I thought,

"Oh that's nice, for someone else, but not for me."

I don't really know why I shirked the possibility so fast, as I do consider myself a very intuitive person. I guess I just didn't understand the *depth* of connection that is possible between mother and child. I understand it now. I had begun to think messages all of the sudden like, "Roxana needs to pee". I questioned these "thoughts" every time saying,

"Oh, no she just went" or "I'll put her on when I'm done".

Time and time again, seconds to minutes after my "thought", Roxana would invariably pee in her little pants. After about the 50th time of ignoring my instincts I started putting her on whenever I "felt" like she had to go. No matter what; I stopped second guessing myself and was absolutely blown away at how accurate these feelings and thoughts were. My mom was visiting us at our home one day and was playing with Roxana while I cooked lunch. All of the sudden I said, "Roxana has to go pee!"

My mom put her on the potty right away and tinkle she went. This phenomenon occurred 4 more times that day and my mom finally asked me what was going on! She couldn't believe how I knew every time. This connection is really *fantastic* and will come to you eventually, even if you are not looking for it. If you are aware and working with your baby you will soon be able to tell when they have to eliminate just as I and many other mothers and parents do.

My intuition spoke to me with a sudden urge to urinate myself but with a picture of Roxana in my head. Sometimes I saw a flash of her needing to go or felt a strong sense of urgency to get to her. Often times just the words, "Roxana has to go pee", would flash into my head. I'm sure it manifests differently in all parents but you will begin to recognize the sensations or messages you get.

Little Bits of Encouragement

Listen to your intuition, it is there to guide you and support you.

Those months of spending quality time together were pure heaven for both of us. Not that it was a breeze, *by any means*, or that everything was dandy but from an animalistic, instinctual perspective we were doing what we needed to do. We created many learning activities, read tons of books, engaged in lots of play and ate delicious, healthy food. Roxana was eating all kinds of things! I was making all of her food homemade. It was so easy. I would buy organic bulk grains and vegetables, keeping meals simple. It would take me a couple hours one day a week to prepare many wonderful instant meals for her. I would steam sweet potatoes, carrots, and peas (all her favorites), and would mash them up separately. I'd keep small dishes of the food fresh in the refrigerator usually about 2 days worth of meals. I'd freeze the remainder in ice cube trays and then transfer them to a little freezer bag for each type of vegetable. I'd have food for the whole week and often into the next week. I could unthaw these and feed them to her straight or mix them in soup. I'd feed her fresh fruits, avocado and other veggies that didn't freeze as well throughout the week.

I only fed Roxana from a store bought jar once and she made a horrible face, she wouldn't eat it and I don't blame her, I tasted it and that stuff was terrible. I introduced her to coconut milk soups and curry; potatoes with dill and mashed garlic and many other distinct tastes. She is not a picky eater and I know it's from the diversity of the food I fed her as well as the quality. She was still breastfeeding also and was just as healthy as could be.

In my opinion, the very best gift a mother can give her baby is her breast milk. The very best gift a father can give his baby is doing anything and everything to support the mother's need to breastfeed. Breast milk cannot be duplicated, *ever*. It is the most amazing substance and is tailored to a baby's specific requirements. To encourage a functioning and strong digestive system... breastfeed, to encourage a sturdy immune system with limited infections and sickness... breastfeed, to encourage brain and body development... breastfeed, to encourage regular and healthy elimination patterns... breastfeed. The longer the better but breastfeeding for *at least* one year is incredibly vital to an infant's overall growth and development. This has been proven over and over and over again, I cannot stress the benefits enough. Breastfeeding creates regular stools and allows a baby to consume only what he/she can readily digest. This is a key element to fostering a healthy elimination process for the body.

As babies get older, the more whole foods you can feed them, the better. I could go on and on about diet and what we feed our children and the rate of child diabetes and all sorts of frightening facts but the point I want to illustrate pertains to PTBT Method. *The healthier your child is and the healthier they eat the easier and more regular their elimination processes will be.* I have dealt with zero digestive issues with Roxana, zero incidents of severe constipation or diarrhea that ever required any kind of concern or medication. Besides, the new food introduction made for some very interesting poops and I was incredibly thankful that Roxana was already using the potty chair so I didn't have to mop up some of those suckers!

10 months to 1 Year:

Roxana was doing very well and learned so much during those months we spent together. One of her favorite things was to walk around the house being held so she could point at everything and be told what things were called. She wanted to absorb her entire environment and she did. She so loved knowing what everything was that her game got to a point where I would ask her,

"Where is the door?" and she'd point to it.

"Where is the door knob? Where is the couch?"

"Where is the ceiling fan? Where is the floor?"

She could go on and on, she knew *where* and *what* surrounded her. She would grin and giggle with delight at her own understanding of her life and what was in it.

Roxana was able to recognize sign language very early and would look to the potty if I signed for it and would reach out for me when I signed for "milk". I kept at it and wondered if she'd ever sign back but at 10 months she began trying to sign herself! She showed me "potty", "milk" and "all done". Her signs were still in their formative stages at that point but she was actively trying to communicate with me and it allowed me the opportunity to stop and try to figure out what she was saying or needing. I was so pleased that Roxana felt as if she had another outlet for communication with me and at 10 months she was giving it a shot!

It was so thrilling, and made our relationship a little more equal. I didn't have to do as much guess work and her needs were met with more ease which reduced her crying. She began using the potty sign I had taught her very regularly. I stopped using the "poop" sign around that time and just decided to streamline all the potty signs into one. I used the sign for "toilet" only, which included pee and poop. "Toilet" was the sign Roxana began showing me when she had to use the bathroom. I did not try any kind of special technique to teach her sign language I just consistently signed to her the words I felt were most important. Roxana was very smart and knew about everything in her environment long before she could verbalize and through sign language she had an opportunity to "talk" back. All babies have this potential.

Her favorites were "milk" and "more"! I saw those signs *a lot*. When Roxana began signing to me our potty training adventure took another turn. It was funny because just as her communication became more intricate she also became very mobile. When potty training got a little easier it also got a little more difficult! What do you know about that, eh? The classic reality of parenthood; as soon as you think you've got something down pat, BOOM, your child changes and its back to the drawing board.

With Roxana's new found mobility she was all over the place and was very involved in her new discoveries. We had hardwood floors in our apartment at the time so she would play with no diaper and if there was an occasional pee accident it wasn't a big deal to clean up. I was offering her the potty in the morning, before and after each nap and before she went to bed. Our bathroom was too small to have the potty chair set up in there without me tripping over it so I'd keep it mainly in our bedroom for ease and availability. Once Roxana became more mobile I'd move the potty chair out to the living room during the day so she could familiarize herself with it and could learn that she had the power to initiate her own use. Sometimes she would crawl to it when she had to go, other times she didn't. It was available for her and in her sights so she knew it was a natural and acceptable part of the day. Her clues and her signing to use the potty were usually very noticeable although sometimes I couldn't tell until too late. More so it was because, as a single mother, I was often cleaning or cooking while she played, always trying to get caught up!

It is useful to keep the *Sweet Seat* on the potty when a child is older and cruising around a lot to keep the bowl in place and minimize playing with the potty chair. Creating accessibility for your child to initiate elimination is needed and important but you must also maintain that the potty chair isn't a toy to be taken apart or a place for toys to be put inside the chair. I let Roxana climb on it and sit on it whenever she wanted but did not let her turn it into a doll house or a hat for her head. With clear and loving communication the child's phase of wanting to take it apart and play with it won't last long. Once your baby is big enough and is actively dumping his/her own pee, remove the padding so the child can access the bowl with ease!

We would often spend the night about once a week over at my mom's during the 8 months Roxana and I lived in Tacoma. I would bring along her potty chair just as I would bring anything else we would need. It was a common part of our lives. I taught my mom and my brothers how to watch for Roxana's signs and how to position her on the potty. They adored her and thought our practice was different and a *little weird* but incredible to watch. They are still Roxana's biggest fans and the feeling is mutual. When I'd bring the potty chair there we would keep it out in the living room as that was where Roxana played the most and usually where we slept. Being that I had the habit of thoroughly cleaning the chair after every pee

and poop, it was sanitary and when placed with all of Roxana's other gear it became a very normal part of everyone's life. When we'd sleep in my mom's room I'd set the chair next to the bed and would lift it up between my legs easily in the morning for her elimination and also be ready for any nighttime needs. I always kept a half roll or smaller sized roll of toilet paper with the potty chair so paper was always accessible.

There were many days that Roxana would only use one diaper and then there were some days that we would go through six. The changes depended on the environment, what we were doing, how she was feeling, all the elements that affect us as humans. I tried to stay calm and optimistic and remember on the days we would go through six diapers what the true point of this whole practice was. It was to help facilitate Roxana's knowledge of herself and her ability to communicate that knowledge. Sometimes it was tough to go a few weeks straight using hardly any diapers then all of the sudden to go through a half a bag. This is where I'd take a step back and reset my initial goals. I would focus on just catching her elimination after wake-ups. I reminded myself that I did not have to worry about every other time during her awake, active playing. This reevaluation worked very well and as soon as I'd back off from my frustration and expectations we would launch back into using a diaper a day.

I was using disposable diapers and cloth diapers at this time. If we stayed home during the day then Roxana would either wear a cloth diaper or more commonly she would be diaper free. During the day she would wear a little t-shirt and a pair of baby leggings pulled all the way up her thigh. I cut all the onesies I had, hemmed the bottoms and made t-shirts from them. The snaps and design of onesies were a pain and too much work for a potty training person; they are definitely created for diaper training babies. This way her genitals were completely free and she was still covered and warm.

Other times she would wear the smallest pair of cotton pants or full coverage leggings I could find. I fashioned some little panties for her also but it was tough because Roxana was so small and slender. Part of my new PTBT Method clothing line includes very small panties for our little ones also skinnier fitting pants. Kid's clothes on the mainstream market made for children less than 2 years old all have *huge* butts and wide waists, built for bulky diapers. Roxana and I had problems finding clothes to fit her and still do with jeans and all things bottom related.

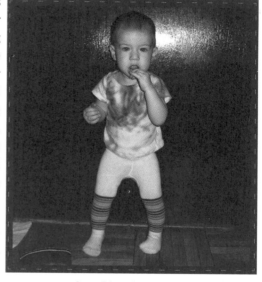

When Roxana wore pants, panties or cloth diapers and she had an accident she would feel it right away as it was very uncomfortable. She would let me know and/or I could tell and I'd change her immediately, decreasing substantially her time spent with any urine burning her sensitive skin. I also began incorporating diaper free night time. I would start out offering her potty time before she fell asleep for the night. When Roxana would urinate before bed she'd sleep through the night, nice and dry. If she was too tired to try to pee I'd skip the potty session and she would usually need to pee within the first couple of hours after falling asleep. After that one pee she would then remain dry for the rest of the night. I'd change her then let her sleep naked until morning. She absolutely loved it! She'd sprawl out like a little "king of the world." Her legs would be stretched out and free of any uncomfortable binding or irritating red indentations the morning after from the diaper being too tight around her body. I can't imagine sleeping in those horrible things.

I was breastfeeding so the natural sleeping arrangement for us was to share a bed. I highly recommend it in the first year. It is very special and once again, they are only babies for a very short time. I had moved to using a cloth diaper with a waterproof cover at night so after a couple of hours I'd reach over and feel to see if the diaper was wet. I also used a "makeshift" bed liner with waterproof pads to lay Roxana on so she wouldn't have to wear a diaper at all. If she peed on them I'd remove the liner and we'd go back to sleep, however, this "makeshift" arrangement was bulky and uncomfortable for me. I liked the idea of her not wearing diapers at all much better but I couldn't maintain it for long. Which is why I developed what I call the *Dry Dreams Bedliner* to make this transition so much easier than it was for me. The runner is long enough to be tucked in tightly on both sides of a king size bed. It is waterproof and absorbent but not bulky so adults can sleep comfortably on it. If the baby pees you just remove the liner and your bed is saved from saturation, everyone can get back to sleep quickly without any undue stress. I wish I would have had it when I was first starting with Roxana, I will certainly use it from the very beginning if I have another baby.

If you decide not to share a bed or have your baby right next to you in his/her own bed you will probably be getting up to nurse or feed your baby anyway so you can check his/her diaper. If the diaper is wet take it off and let him/her sleep naked for the rest of the night. Roxana's crib mattress was fitted with a waterproof sheet, those are easy to find. She sleeps on her crib mattress now, taken out of the crib and positioned up next to my bed. I can use the liner on my bed for when she sleeps with me but I usually end up moving her over to her space in the middle of the night so we can sleep a little bit more soundly. Either way you have insurance and that feels great to know you are doing the right thing for your baby and that you are physically supported in your choice.

This is also why I encourage people, when starting PTBT Method, to focus only on the poop, once you get that down it really changes everything. Dealing with urine is so much easier in many ways than with feces. By the time Roxana turned a year old, she had only pooped in a diaper ten times since I began sitting her on the potty chair at 3 months old. So if you break it down time-wise, for approximately nine months she averaged less than one poop in a diaper per month! My goal was by far exceeded! Yowza, we were really learning and growing together!

13 months to 18 months:

When Roxana turned a year old my plan was to get back to work. By her birthday in April, I had exhausted all of my credit cards and was down to my last $1,500. I had still not received any financial assistance or child support from Roxana's dad so that was something I couldn't count on. I had been searching for jobs for a few months and had run across a position working for a beekeeper and selling honey in Seattle. It sounded so lovely; I had always been incredibly intrigued by bees and was definitely a fan of honey! However, the ad was for very part time work, I would not be making much and I would need to move again, to Seattle. I sort of held the idea on the back burner and was feeling a lot of pressure to conform to my societal duties, if you will. I was trained in a number of different areas and had held several interesting and high paying jobs. My last big money maker was working as a corporate flight attendant where I flew all over the world on private jets. Nice gig, but I would need *total* flexibility so that was out of the question.

I figured getting a job as a waitress to start would be logical, easy, non-committal and in the state of Washington you can make decent money. We have the highest minimum wage at about $8.75 an hour plus tips. However, I didn't *want* to do the rational more reasonable thing, I didn't *want* to stay where I was and start waitressing, it just didn't fit me. I sat in my apartment and held both ideas in my heart, waitressing and being logical or selling honey and being illogical. My body would physically warm up when I thought about selling honey and I felt it was my path so that's just what I did. There I go again, following my intuition...

Roxana and I moved a couple of weeks after her birthday up to north Seattle in a neighborhood called Ballard where I found a great apartment and I started working. I received my first child support payment from Roxana's dad in June so that was a relief and I had a lot of great ideas for the honey business. My boss took in all my suggestions and we started off with gusto! My very part time work turned into a full time job where I worked out of the house half the week and worked from the home the other half. Roxana was spending 3 days per week at my girlfriend Laura's house just down the

street. She was privy to the potty training Roxana and I were practicing so Laura would put her on the potty after she woke up from her naps. She was watching for Roxana's sign language and she'd ask her and offer other potty opportunities as well throughout the day.

She did very well over there even though Laura didn't give her the kind of diaper free time that I did at home because she had a little girl still in diapers also and it was kind of a handful. Roxana's dad began staying at my apartment every other weekend in order for him to spend time with her and so I could get in a few more days of work. I showed him what was going on, he had seen it in the beginning as well but had been absent from our progression. Roxana would typically have more accidents with her dad than she would anywhere else. I would experience maybe one or two accidents in a week and a half and then she'd have 3 or 4 during the weekend that they were together. I think he wasn't used to being with a child for several hours straight and was more focused on playing and not on what her physical needs were.

My mom also watched Roxana occasionally while I worked and I would bring her down to my mom's house for overnight visits. She did well there and had very few accidents (meaning she actually peed in a diaper). It is very important to communicate clearly with all of the people involved in raising your child. The practice of putting a baby on a potty chair to eliminate is not difficult; really the biggest step is the adult needing to change their perspective and once that happens it can be smooth sailing.

In our new place we had a bigger bathroom and Roxana was at the age that she could walk to it so I decided to set up her potty chair in the bathroom with mine. Around 13 months she began saying, "POOP!" and would run towards the bathroom. She'd yell this for both poop and pee and would simultaneously show her "toilet" sign. This was her habit for nearly three months. It was funny because Roxana was already using a few other words like, "mama", "up", "this", "that" and "done". She knew the difference between pee and poop, it was as if she thought it was *hilarious* to yell poop!

I loved our new apartment but I was bummed about the fact that we had carpet. Her habit of running to the bathroom would sometimes lead to a long trail of urine on the carpet. The first few months we lived there I felt like I was doing a lot of cleaning up. It was frustrating for me and I know it was more difficult because I was working a lot and then coming home and, still being a single parent, I had to take care of everything. It is a tough job and although I have had a smashing success with it, I would never want to be a single parent again! Oh well, I am a firm believer in *Simple Green* so I had a bottle armed and ready when needed.

Roxana had been doing so well with pooping that really the only messes I had to clean up were pee and then it started to change. She pooped a few times when her dad was over, and then it began to happen more. She'd yell poop and try to make it to the bathroom and instead of a urine trail I had a shit trail! *Oh God*... There were a few weeks there that I almost gave up. I was so busy and exhausted from long days and long nights I began thinking,

"We did well and I am happy how far we've come but I'm just too busy to keep doing this. I'll put her back in a diaper and we'll be done."

Of course that never happened because I couldn't do that to her. She would have been very confused and incredibly uncomfortable. Also when compared to the amount of poop cleaning up that I actually had to do it was probably 1/16th of what diaper trained children require. I was spoiled in many ways. I realize that some of you are probably thinking,

"Ya, but the poop was on your carpet, not in a diaper!!!"

You are right, it was and I had to get on my hands and knees and scrub it up. But check this out... How many of us have pets? How many people are totally willing, without a second thought, to get a puppy or a kitten? Both of these animals are often kept inside at least for a good portion of their lives if not for the entire thing. Both require potty training or need to be "house broken." We are willing to mop up dog and cat poop from our carpets, our couches, our clothes. And cat urine smells far worse than baby urine.

Doesn't it seem a little backwards and weird when you think of it this way? Why do we deny the opportunity to train our babies the same way? It would *not* be very effective to train our animals to *not* poop on the floor by cramming them into a diaper. It makes more sense to leave their bodies in a natural state, to communicate with them clearly and to clean up when they make mistakes. If we can give this respect and love to our pets during their early stages can't we at least offer the same opportunity to our children? Anyway, the pooping on the floor stopped and she was able to get to the potty on time. It was a brief period and I am so grateful that I didn't panic and become so discouraged that I gave up our practice or held it against her or myself for "failing".

Little Bits of
Encouragement

Cultivate compassion for your baby's new journey and your own path as a parent. We are only human!

From the point that we moved into our new apartment to Roxana's 18 month birthday I purchased three bags of disposable diapers. We still had several left and Roxana used them to diaper her dolls for over a year until I finally got rid of them. I would add one diaper to Roxana's bag for going down to Laura's, she would put it on her for naps but was beginning to phase them out as Roxana was doing so well and I had asked her to try more diaper free time when she was comfortable with it. I hadn't been making her wear a diaper for naps for several months at home because she was always dry and I wanted her to have more sleep time that was free of constraint.

I'd send two or three diapers down to my mom's house when Roxana would spend the night. For awhile she'd come back with zero but then I began sending only one diaper and sure enough, that was plenty. My mom really only used the diaper for overnight and naps so her bed wouldn't get peed on. Roxana was always dry in the morning so she could continue to use the same diaper at other points in the day if she needed to. As far as wipes went, I used one wipe per poop after I did the bulk of wiping with toilet paper and I never used them for pee. This gave her a smooth, soft finish and insured that I got everything. Their little butts are so sensitive I didn't want her feeling like it hurt to be wiped. I continued this until she was two and never bought them again.

We were at a point at home that I only put a diaper on her sometimes at night and when we went in the car. I would always ask her to use the bathroom before we left, which we did together, as it's a good idea for everyone! But I still put a diaper on her because that was a mess I didn't want to deal with. I would carry the potty chair with us in the back of the car. Not for quick trips but when we would venture to my mom's house or out to my dad's farm for a visit, both places being one to three hours away.

I set it up in the back in a comfortable flat position with a toilet paper roll in the bowl for easy access. This way, when I needed to stop for Roxana, I could pull over virtually anywhere and could sit her right up on the potty. She usually went pee, I can only think of one time during that phase that she pooped. When she peed I'd just dump the pee on the ground and I'd save the little piece of toilet paper I wiped her with in a little bag or I'd put it in the bowl after it was empty. When she pooped I just covered it with toilet paper and when I got to a gas station I took out the bowl and dumped it in the toilet, gave it a quick clean and we were on our way!

Roxana had been telling me when she had to go potty while we were driving for months. First she was using her "potty" sign then she would say her favorite, "poop!" She had accidents, especially when she'd fall asleep on a longer trip but they were becoming fewer and fewer. I started taking the diaper off sometimes for the second half of the trip if she'd just gone pee. It was nerve racking so I created another "makeshift" waterproof pad she could sit on and it made it so much better. I didn't have to worry about getting the car seat soaking wet. I also designed and have available the *Ellie Pad* which is specifically made to fit car seats but is fashioned to be multi functional as well. This pad will make your experience far less fretful and much more simplified than mine was. I love it and once again I wish I had it when I was potty training Roxana...next time!

In October just before Roxana's 18 month mark we took a trip to Portland which was three hours from my apartment to my girlfriend's front door. On that trip Roxana took our training to the last level. She informed me that she had to go pee; I pulled over and put her on our "traveling potty chair" in the back of the car. When she was done I was about to put another diaper on her because we still had a long way to go and she said,

"No mama, Dada done."

Saying Roxana is tough, so for several months she called herself Dada, for Xana. She referred to herself in third person about everything, it was ridiculously cute.

"Dada wants an apple," "Dada is tired," "Dada loves you."

She learned to say her name before she was two and would introduce herself as, not only Roxana, but *Roxana Josephine*. She has zero issues with pronouncing her name now.

I asked her if she was sure she was done wearing diapers, to clarify what was going on and she said,

"No more, mama."

So I left the diaper off her. I told her if I was going to let her ride without her diaper she had to make *sure* she told me when she had to go pee. I told her it was *not ok* to pee in her seat. She said ok and off we went. During that car trip Roxana told me three times that she had to pee. We'd pull over and she would relieve herself in her potty chair stationed in the back of the car. It was a great and surprise success!

That was it, from that trip on I made sure I had her potty set up in the back, that I had my water proof padding just in case and I would ask her fairly often if she needed to go. I'd usually get a, "no, mom" answer but I asked anyway. She'd tell me when she had to go and from that point, when she was 18 months until now, well over a year later, she's probably had four accidents. We were officially done with all daytime diapers! Yay!! It seemed at points that practicing PTBT Method was strenuous and time consuming but then at other times it was the easiest and most natural thing to do. And then there I was, all of the sudden, with a potty trained 1 ½ year old! I was done, she was done. I never put another diaper on her during the day.

19 Months to Present:

I carried the potty chair in the back of the car on our longer journeys until just before her 2nd birthday. By then Roxana was a pro and we could use any bathroom along the way. She was also very good at holding it until I got to the nearest restroom. I would explain to her that it was really important to tell me as soon as she felt like she had to pee and not to wait to tell me. I also told her how to squeeze her vagina to keep the pee in. She thought this was very funny and got a kick out of practicing holding it until we stopped.

Never make your children wait for long!!! Making children wait to pee when they have to go has horribly negative effects on the urinary tract system and the bladder's functionality. Not to mention the psychological damage from embarrassment and/or punishment that would come from an accident. At 2 ½ years old, if we were to go on a very long trip, over five hours, I'd bring the potty chair along. Or if we go camping or anywhere far out of the city I bring the potty chair just to have something warm and safe in the car for any night driving or any emergency situations. It's not a bad idea to keep the potty chair around on adventures until your child becomes acclimated to pooping outside and in several different types of environments. It is better to keep your children feeling safe and secure than to rush them into being too grown up too fast. They are still very little people and outhouses can be freaky for anyone!

Once Roxana was fully potty trained I would also carry an extra set of pants, panties and socks around with me wherever we'd go. By 2 years old I pretty much stopped doing this although I still think it's a good idea and will bring extras of everything along for full day trips because kids are kids! She could get just as wet at the beach playing in the water and sand or sitting in a melting ice-cream cone as she could if she had an accident. I definitely didn't stress about it and being prepared always makes the unexpected a little easier to swallow.

Things were going well after we finished with daytime diapers, an occasional accident of pee on the floor happened here and there but *no diapers* were *no problem*! About a month later when Roxana was 19 months old she and I talked and decided she was done with diapers at night too. We just had to make sure she went

pee before bed and then we were usually good to go. We worked on her waking me up in the night if she had to go by reminding her every night a few times before we went to sleep. I am glad we did this because as she got older she needed to pee more in the middle of the night.

As I mentioned before, Roxana sleeps on her little bed next to mine and sometimes still crawls over to snuggle with me. She is very good at waking up and saying,

"Mom, I have to pee" in the middle of the night but there are times that I ask her because her restlessness wakes me up.

You can tell when a child has to urinate as the need typically wakes him/her up enough that the child starts moving around a lot. Sighing and trying to reposition themselves is very common. This movement may not wake them up enough that they become conscious and tell you they have to go, so if you notice it I encourage you to ask them. I would and still do say,

"Roxana, do you have to pee?"

Usually she says yes although there are times she says no and if she doesn't answer at all I tell her,

"I am taking you to the potty because I think you have to pee."

Clear communication is important in the middle of the night. Your child could be dreaming and not fully waken until they are on the potty and the change could scare them. Always talk to your kids about what you are doing and what they are doing as far as elimination is concerned.

We have had a handful of accidents overnight from 19 months to almost 3 years old but they are few and far between. I take it as a process, nothing is perfect and accidents happen. There were months when we'd go with none or one accident per month then all of the sudden multiple accidents would occur. When Roxana was a little over 2 years old she peed in my bed twice, my mom's once and twice at my dad's all in one week! I was going to pull my hair out. I kept talking to her about it, asking her why she wasn't waking up and telling me. I told her she couldn't do it again or I wasn't sure what we were going to have to do. Maybe go back to diapers, she literally laughed and said,

"No, mom." And then that was it, no more accidents.

Our children are constantly going through growth spurts; it can affect them in so many ways. I assume that is what that week was; maybe she had a lot of hormones going through her. She was eating more, her legs were hurting and she needed a deeper, longer sleep, making it hard for her to wake up. It is our job to recognize our children's growth patterns and to be patient and loving with all the changes.

I had been working full-time from our move to Seattle until just before Roxana turned 2 ½. My job had really taken off and I had been instrumental in the growth of the business. I had gone from a very part time gig making very little money to managing 13 people and running the business. I really busted my ass for that company and it paid off. I had entered into the work force again with a staggering $32,000 in debt. This debt was *not* from hanging with my girlfriends and drinking martinis in gold plated glasses. It was from purchasing a car, a basic computer and from living expenses while I stayed home with my daughter.

Through hard work, focus and faith I was able to get *entirely out of credit card debt within one year* of the first payment I made. I had trusted my instinct to be with my daughter when it was vital for us both. I believed in my intuition when it went against everything that made sense. I was given a gift from the universe but I also acted on that gift, I worked long hours and dedicated myself to my goals. Not only did I dissolve $32,000 in debt in one year but I did it as a single mother and I did it in a failing economy. Anything can be accomplished if you want it bad enough and you practice the delicate balance of letting the heart guide the head.

Roxana had a nanny, Bee, during those several months that I worked during high season that came to our house and watched her a few days a week and then she spent the rest of the week at Laura's. Both women did phenomenal jobs working with Roxana through the PTBT Method. It was often that, Roxana's "best friend", her nanny "Aunt Bee" would thank me profusely for working with Roxana as early as I had on potty training as Bee had seen some poops coming from that little girl that she did not want to mess around with! Obviously, having a child potty trained makes it astronomically easier for all caretakers to watch over your child. Everybody appreciates not having to mop up smashed, hot poop from a diaper.

Roxana and I began a sticker system when she was around 2 ½, I recommend using reinforcements *only* when the child has already completed potty training. Do not use them for babies and early toddlers and never for the "act" of eliminating only for the correct *placement* of bodily waste. I did not give Roxana stickers because she pooped when I wanted her to; I gave her stickers because she pooped on her own time, *in the big potty*. This exercise was a counting exercise, a lesson in attention and tracking, she practiced writing numbers, letters and making shapes on her sticker board.

We used this system for about two months then using the big potty for poops became her regular thing. We never talked about it ending, it just sort of slipped away and I will still occasionally surprise her with a little pack of stickers for being such a great child and for using the toilet like a big girl all the time. I've thought of getting rid of her potty chair but have decided against it for now as we only have one bathroom and her and I often have to pee at the same time. It's nice to have an extra toilet in the house and it stays clean and non invasive since all I have to do is dump the pee and rinse the pot and we're on our way!

As I write this book my daughter runs around, plays, eats, sings, dances and develops the most amazing imaginative stories. She called to me a few minutes ago and said,

"Mom, I have to poop now."

I said, "Ok, get in there" and I followed her in.

She put her stool against the bottom of the regular toilet and climbed up all by herself. She asked me to turn the fan on. I walked out to write some more and about two minutes later she yelled,

"I'm all done mama!" So I went back in to help her wipe.

She said, "Don't forget to write up a number mom."

We are keeping track of her poops on the big potty; every time she poops three in a row she gets a package of stickers. I said ok and wrote a number two on the page.

She said, "I am getting sooo many stickers!"

As I was wiping her she turned and looked into the toilet. She said,

"Oh, look! A mama, a papa and a baby poop!"

As there were three poops, all different sizes in the toilet. She said,

"A whole family at the park, they all went to the park together. The potty park, mom; now isn't that nice?"

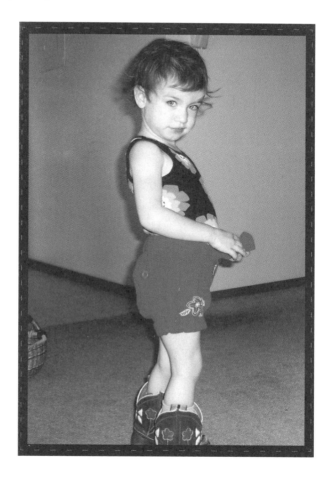

This is my wonderful little girl and I could not be more proud!

PTBT Method–

Wisdom from the Past to Better Our Future

A Step by Step Guide to Establishing Intuition, Self Esteem and a Healthy Body

1.) Start As Early As Possible:

Relax the first month; give yourself time to get adjusted to your new baby. Spend those first precious weeks watching, loving and nursing your baby. After a month, infants begin to eliminate with more regularity making this a great time to start. You can begin later, really at any time, but starting at one month is going to give you the greatest advantage as you have not spent a lot of time training your baby to use diapers. The earlier you start paying attention the better.

2.) Determine The Goal:

One of the key factors of success with this is setting a small goal and gradually building from that, then whenever you hit a tough spot revert back to the initial goal and start again. This way you have a very easy and relaxed methodology to follow and you will not butt your head against a wall trying to perfect anything or forget that your baby is, well... *a baby*!

I decided that catching my daughter's poop would be my focal point. I figured learning her pee schedule would be much more difficult to nail down. I narrowed my focal point into the simple, stress free goal of catching just her morning poop. One a day, that was it. I thought if I could just tune in enough to be there for her morning poop (which came nearly every day) then I'd be satisfied.

Please realize that any amount of effort that you put into working with your infant is beneficial. The bond alone is something worth the effort. Take time to get used to everything especially if you've had previous children and diaper trained them. The PTBT Method is just as easy and convenient as packing your baby into a diaper but it is very different. You will spend your time and energy in opposite ways than you would with diaper training infants.

Keep your goals realistic, small and easy. I began with that minimalistic goal and a couple of times through the first few months found myself reverting back to that simple starting point. For the most part, though, Roxana caught on and so did I and the next thing we knew we were way ahead of my goal. The point is to never lose sight of the simplicity, even when your baby begins to blow you away with his/her awareness and abilities. Always go back to the beginning if you ever start feeling frustrated or impatient.

3.) Watch For Signs:

Begin watching your baby for his/her physical and verbal signs that he/she has to go to the bathroom. When your baby poops it'll be much more obvious than when he/she is peeing. Signs can be little cries or whimpers, reddening of the face, moans, grunts, and physical movements either very increased and/or very still. Wiggling, narrowing of the eyebrows and very concentrated looks are all common. Every child is different but these basic examples will cover most of the behaviors babies demonstrate before going to the bathroom. Familiarize yourself with these signs.

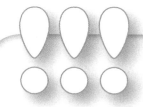

Common Elimination Signals

- whimpering
- grunting
- red face
- straining
- wiggling like a worm

- looks of concentration
- narrowing of eyebrows
- soft moaning and crying
- sudden increased movement or suddenly very still

4.) Create Verbal Cue:

Decide on a verbal cue. Once you decide, please keep it the same so you don't confuse your baby. This technique is very powerful and it is vital that you maintain a consistent and obvious cue for your baby. I chose to use a "pssst" sound for both peeing and pooping as it simplified things for me. Also when Roxana would really be working on pooping I would moan a bit, softly grunting and breathing deep to encourage her to breathe and to empathize with her if it was a little tough or a bit of a struggle. Some babies and kids don't like to poop and can create a fear of it if it hurts their little butts. I believe by creating a feeling of empathy and experiencing it with your baby it encourages him/her to keep going and also evokes the feeling that pooping has a natural *progression* to it. It takes time and is not meant to be pushed out in one big painful grunt, very similar to birthing, actually. He/she is doing the right thing by getting it out with patience and with breath.

All of the infant potty training books I read discuss the use of verbal cues which are made by the parents as the baby urinates or poops. Everyone has different variations on it but all of them use it. I highly recommend using the same cue and actions I use for the PTBT Method, however, if it is more natural for you to use another sound, do it. Come up with something that is easily associated with the act of going to the bathroom. You don't want a cue like "lalalala" or "chuggachugga" it needs to be something that draws the natural conclusion that it is potty time not play time. Using a sound that stimulates the elimination process is the key element. Often times turning on running water makes people feel like they have to urinate. This is why I established the "pssst" sound as the recommended cue. Also, the soft grunting and moaning cue for pooping is associated with pushing and the physical body immediately begins to copy the sound.

5.) Sit Baby Up:

Once you have determined your baby's signals it is time to take the physical action of sitting your baby up for pooping. Whenever you see your babies sign, sit him/her up propped in your lap with his/her back on your thighs. Lean against a wall with your knees up and bent and your feet flat on the ground. Or sit on a couch with your feet on a high stool and your knees up to create a nice comfortable seat for your baby. This position is best because you can look  at each other and talk, laugh, sing and have fun as well as communicate very clearly what is going on. Your baby will not have fear because he/she is facing you and is protected by your body.

Try this position for one week with the diaper *still on* before removing it and letting your baby eliminate into the potty chair. This way you both get accustomed to the new routine and it is a comfortable and safe experience for you both. There is no pressure or worry about positioning your baby correctly or any poop and pee spraying out. He/she will need an adjustment period to get used to eliminating while sitting up and if you are starting at one month old your baby needs to be additionally supported by your hands. Allow yourself the time to get acclimated and you both will smoothly move to the next step. His/her little body will appreciate the gesture; also make sure the diaper isn't too tight, your baby needs to sit up comfortably without the diaper squeezing his/her stomach.

My daughter responded very well to this and never pooped lying down again. I believe using gravity and putting your baby in the correct position for all natural human elimination as soon as possible will only benefit him/her. It starts the infant on the right track and reduces confusion about how to go to the bathroom. This position also helps with the body's ability to physically eliminate effectively. The body is not fighting gravity and it has a clear open channel to release toxins from the system. This is why I made sitting your baby up a vital part of the PTBT Method.

As Roxana and I developed our communication and routine we always used both physical positioning and verbal cues together when she relieved herself. Being that she was in the obvious and natural position for elimination Roxana began peeing nearly every time she pooped. Once I transferred her to the potty chair I inadvertently began to catch most of her pee as well! What a deal!

6.) Communicate With Baby:

Now that you recognize your baby's signs, you are sitting the child up on your legs and you are making the cue noise as the baby eliminates, you can begin fully communicating. While your baby is eliminating, whether it is pee or poop, actively make the cue noise you've chosen. Also, while eliminating talk with your little one about what he/she is doing. You can say;

"Oh, you are going poop"

"Push it out, breathe it out"

"You're sitting up to go poop"

"Nice job going pee in the potty!"

Telling your baby exactly what he/she is doing is hugely important. Your baby is absorbing everything you say and it encourages your baby to become very aware of his/her bodily sensations and the correct verbiage for those sensations.

Next add sign language to your communication smorgasbord! Show your baby the ASL sign for toilet while talking with him/her, sign to the child and say poop simultaneously. This plethora of information given to a baby is the perfect way to validate and explain what he/she is experiencing. I find it incredibly important to give children as much information as possible.

Being able to feel body function, hear correct terminology and see imagery all at once increases the brain's ability to sustain information. These techniques help to sear new ideas into anybody's brain, whether adult, child or baby. Within the PTBT Method, the infant physically feels the waste coming from his/her body, the baby hears you make cue sounds and instinctually connects them with the physical sensations the baby feels. He/she also hears the correct terminology for what is happening and the infant will see you

Open and close your hand a few times, like you are squeezing. Always say Milk simultaneously.

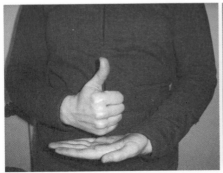 

Begin with hands low to the waist and raise them up to chest. Always say Help simultaneously.

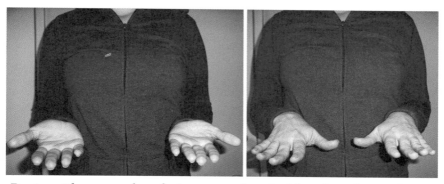

Begin with your palms facing up and end with palms facing down.
Repeat a few times. Always say All Done simultaneously.

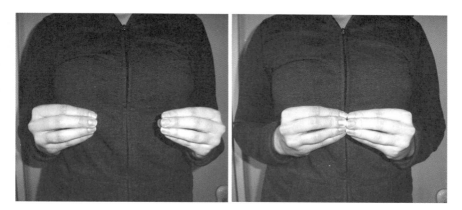

Move your fingers together and apart a few times.
Always say More simultaneously.

Create the sign for T and rotate your wrist back and forth. Always say Potty simultaneously.

showing him/her the nonverbal words. The combination of sensory awareness and information allows children to recognize the connection between the *initial* feelings in their body and the final, physical act of eliminating. This helps children to become more aware of their functions and teaches them to trust their body's feelings and instincts.

It makes perfect sense, anytime you take the time to pay attention on a multitude of levels and with a multitude of senses the experience becomes a more profound memory. Imagine as a child baking with your grandmother, she let you feel and roll the dough, you saw the ingredients and the bowls and rolling pin, you smelled the bread baking in the oven, you felt the heat of the warm bread and you tasted the incredible final product! For many of us, experiences like these stay in our memories stronger and longer than other experiences from our childhood. A number of different *sense* experiences bring the memory back; like you walk into a bakery and the smell whisks you away into your grandmothers kitchen, or you unpack the old bowls you used or the crunchy feel of warm bread. All of these separate sense experiences create a whole picture.

When I would sign to Roxana, "potty" that physical sign reminded her of her whole experience and she remembered what it all means together. Or when she saw her potty chair or heard me make the cue sound, each separate action brought the pooping/peeing experience together and if she had to go, she would.

7.) Praise Your Baby:

When your baby finishes going potty, whether pee or poop, give tremendous praise. I would clap and say,

"Great job going pee and poop. Good girl, yay!"

"You did such a super job!"

At the same time as I spoke these words I would also do the signs for them. Praise goes a long way and is one of my most important lessons. It feels good to everyone to know you did something right or well. If you think about infants there is not a whole lot they can do on their own. They have these tiny bodies sporting capable brains that are just soaking up their environments.

All the information around them is absorbed but they cannot write about it, talk to you about it or get up and dance around. They can't hold things or skip through the house. They have to wait to feel the experience of accomplishment for a fair amount of time.

I was amazed when Roxana would poop or pee or both and I would give her praise, her entire face showed pride and a sense of accomplishment. She would grin and her eyes would light up and she really would almost hold herself taller. It was phenomenal. She was doing something. Really doing something all her own and she was getting enormous attention and praise for her actions, she was beside herself. This was a surprise addition to our experience and when I first saw it I couldn't believe it then it began to make so much sense to me. It is never too early or late, for that matter, to make people feel good about what they can do and achieve. Infants have far more going on than we will ever know, by tapping into their experiences we can learn more and more about what they are feeling and communicating. Fascinating!

Little Bits of Encouragement

Believe in your baby and yourself, allowing your natural abilities to bloom.

When Roxana used the potty whether it be pee/poop or both I gave her enormous praise about what she did, when she didn't go or she went in her diaper I did not say anything at all. I would change her or take her off the potty and move on. There was never any disappointment or negative comments, tones, looks or actions. I implore you, as the parents or caretakers of these infants to never behave negatively towards them when they do not perform the way you want them to. As I stated previously, if you begin to feel frustrated and find yourself demanding more, you must go back to your original goal. Trust me that your baby is responding to his/her natural instincts and that with consistency and love from you, he/she will blossom far more than you expect.

8.) The Transfer/Potty Station:

After you have established a familiar behavior pattern and routine with your infant you can then transfer the baby to actually sitting on the potty chair. Position your baby in the same way you have been only put the chair between your legs and remove the diaper so that he/she will eliminate into the chair. Make it seem like a wonderful thing to do, something big girls and boys do.

You can say,

"Yay, this is so exciting, using the potty like a big girl!"

"Wow, you are so good at going poop and pee, you get to use the big potty."

"Great, now you don't have to get poop all over your butt, doesn't that feel so good?"

"No more diapers for you, big boy!"

Also, reassure them about the change,

"Mommy has you."

"Papa will hold you until you're all done going poop in the big potty."

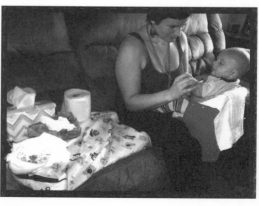

There is no reason in the world that you cannot talk to your infant like he/she understands every word. The more you treat your baby like he/she gets it, the faster your baby will actually get it.

Next, create a potty station. You will need a diaper, wipes, toilet paper and a little plastic bag for garbage. Make an open space for laying him/her down by your side. After your baby eliminates and you have wiped him/her up you need this space for your baby to rest while you remove the potty chair from your legs. If you have a station set up it will be much easier to get your baby in and out of "potty time" and will alleviate the need to scramble around on the fly.

9.) Clean Up:

This is where your potty station comes in handy. After your baby finishes eliminating, you lift the baby and sort of hang him/her on your shoulder while you wipe from behind with toilet paper. When finished wiping with toilet paper dispose of it in the potty bowl. If they only pee then this is the only wiping step you need. If there is poop, then dispose of the toilet paper and grab a baby wipe. You should be able to use one wipe and one only. I would say 90% of the time we used just one, and then there were those rare

occasions that we needed two. I continued to use wipes for finishing up until Roxana was 2 years old, just because her little bottom is so sensitive that I didn't want her to ever feel like the wiping part hurt and have that discourage her potty use. I did, however, use toilet paper for most of poop removal and saved the wipe for a soft finish.

Once you have used the baby wipe or wipes you dispose of them in your little plastic bag or small trash can that is positioned in your potty station. You do not want to add the wipe to the potty bowl as it is not environmentally wise. These things are typically not biodegradable and some carry many additives for scent, moisture and softness making them chemically harmful. You can find additive free wipes on the market now or if you are inclined to use a little soft damp rag or make your own natural baby wipes I highly encourage it. I did not do that this time around but probably will if I ever have another baby.

Now that your baby's butt is all clean and fresh you lay the baby on the floor, bed or couch next to you, on the opposite side of where you have the wipes and other materials. Then remove the potty chair from between your legs. At this point you can turn and re-diaper but there is no real need as your baby just went potty and will not need to go for quite awhile. This is the perfect time to allow a little diaper free time while you get the potty chair all cleaned. Whether you've chosen to diaper or give them "air" time, make sure they are now safely on the ground and in their play area.

Take the potty bowl to the bathroom and *always* add a little water to the potty whether it is pee or poop before you dump it out in the toilet. This adds more liquid and gets everything flowing around better. It makes it very easy to transfer the goods and minimizes the scrubbing needed. After the first deposit, I then rinse until all fragments of poop are out, then squirt a little soap in the bowl and scrub it clean. You can use a little scrub pad but I never had to; I would just make the water very hot and use my hand. As I mentioned already, if you add water to the bowl before dumping of the "goods" then you will have a relatively clean starting point.

I got into the habit of cleaning the bowl this way and it made it so much more convenient and very quick, this way your potty chair is always clean and sanitary so you never have to worry. If you do not wash with soap and water after a pee and only pour it out, the urine will build up on the bowl  and make more work later on. I highly recommend keeping things fresh and sanitary, it takes literally seconds to complete.

10.) Establish Routine:

When I say "routine" I mean whatever you two create for yourselves, what works for your child and lifestyle. When I say "schedule" I mean offering opportunities on a regular basis. I *do not* mean expecting your baby to poop or pee every time you put him/her on the potty or expecting your baby to follow a timed guideline. Potty "opportunities" is a good way to think of using the potty. Remember that your child will know when he/she has to go and you *cannot* force anyone to pee or poop on command.

At this point your baby will have been using the potty at varying times, maybe once a day, maybe more, maybe only when you see obvious signs of need. I now suggest you create a definitive routine and follow daily. First create a routine of potty use after waking, both in the morning and after naps. This can be followed easily by anyone watching or caring for your infant. Nearly all babies, infants, children and adults need to urinate directly after waking and for a healthy bladder, really *should* be going as soon as possible after waking.

Once you get used to the routine and are consistent, add more opportunities. For instance I began putting Roxana on the potty first thing in the morning, *then* I added after naps, *then* I added before and after meals, *then* before and after we left for an outing. I did not try to do everything at once. It may seem like a lot and a bit overwhelming but you will be amazed at how simple it all becomes and when you start using one diaper a day, you will relish in your new found way of life! Your baby will too!

Sticking with a practical routine of pottying after wake-ups, before you leave the house, before and after eating you will find that your schedule is highly effective and your child will fill in the blanks. You must continue to teach and encourage their communication and "listen" to them. In my experience, an additional benefit to the routine was that Roxana would try to poop whenever I put her on the potty even if she didn't have to. She learned that it was a chance to go so she'd give it her best.

There were times when Roxana had to go potty outside of her routine and she would communicate those needs, but for the most part she would stick to the routine because the routine wasn't generated out of nothing, it was based on logic and physical need so it was very natural. I didn't have to worry all day about if she was going to poop or not and if I'd be able to catch

it. The routine creates an ease and a flow to the whole process, less worry for the caretaker and less worry for the infant.

Continue to follow all of the steps I've outlined as your infant grows to be a toddler and on. You have established a routine so stick with it. They are familiar with the process so keep talking to them about it. Update your communication with talk about the new routine,

"Ok let's try to go potty because you just woke up."

"Try to go potty before we leave so we don't have to go in the car!"

"Time for lunch; let's use the potty and wash our hands."

They get it, even if it seems like they don't. Never stop telling them what is going on. As your baby grows their ability to communicate back will advance; first Roxana would show me with her bodily movements and expressions, then she began to look at or move towards the potty, then it was sign language then she would yell "poop" and toddle towards the potty!

There will be more "accidents" when babies grow into toddlerhood as they are very mobile and want to play for longer periods. If you feel your little one is having a difficult time getting to the potty in time please bring it out where he/she can access it easily. Right in the play room works great. Remember that you are dealing with an age that children are generally very willing to do and try what their parents suggest. Once they reach 2 and 3 years old they begin to recognize their independence and want to refuse parental suggestion. I highly recommend spending the time working with your infants and babies so you both can avoid any unpleasantness due to late potty training and extensive diaper training. Stay patient and focus on the simple routine.

11.) The Rules:

The only "rules" I have for PTBT Method are *consistency* and *positive feedback*. Consistency is one of the most important factors of parenting all-together. We all know children learn, follow direction, trust themselves and you more when they have consistent parenting. It is the same with PTBT Method, once you create your schedule and routine keep to it, don't make your baby wear diapers all day and night for two weeks after he/she's been eliminating in a potty. Your baby will be very confused.

I accentuate starting simple and always returning to your original goals when frustrated or, as in my case being a single mother, hugely stressed. If you find yourself in this type of situation and you feel overwhelmed, try offering potty time only after wake-ups. At least your baby will be able to eliminate comfortably upon first waking and when the need feels the most urgent.

I suggest parents refrain from beginning PTBT Method if you feel it is a process you don't want to follow through with. Please wait until you are ready to partake in this wonderful communication so as to minimize frustration and confusion for both baby and parent. With that being said, babies and parents will both benefit greatly from all aspects of this program. If you have a lifestyle that makes you question how well you'll do then I suggest keeping your practice simple. I urge you to stay with the basics and only focus on one poop per day, or one potty opportunity per day.

Keep offering at the same time (time is general; I *do not* mean 7 o' clock every morning I mean whenever the baby first wakes up regardless of the time of day), keep doing the very minimum *every* day. In my estimation, once you get started you will be so floored by the results and your baby will be so happy about not messing itself you will want to dig deeper into the method. These ideas, suggestions and techniques worked for my daughter and me and there is no reason why they wouldn't work for you. I am a big believer in finding your own personal style and that of your infant/child.

Do what works, do what feels right, the only aspects that must very firmly be followed are *consistency* and *positive feedback*. Never say anything negative or degrading to your infant if they do not use the potty when you want them to. The point is to teach them *where* feces/urine belongs, it is to show them how to sit upright and to release, and it is to encourage them to try. *It is not a race, it is not a power struggle, and it is not a competition*. Realize that no matter what level is accomplished with your baby, the communication and positive feedback that was established is a major stepping stone for self-esteem and personal security in your child.

I saw this all the time with Roxana as she projected personal achievement and a sense of accomplishment. She showed ecstatic behavior and great pride in her abilities, it was hilarious and dynamic to watch. It felt good to both of us to get into the habit of positive feedback; I don't believe people practice this enough with each other, in general. It is a wonderful habit to create. Roxana developed an ease with communicating and a very strong sense of trust towards me and others. Her experience was so positive it never gave her any reason to fear or cower to new things. She can be shy sometimes but she is very instinctual and a deep thinker, I believe she likes to scope out situations before she dives right in. Once she dives, well let's just say she swims like a fish!

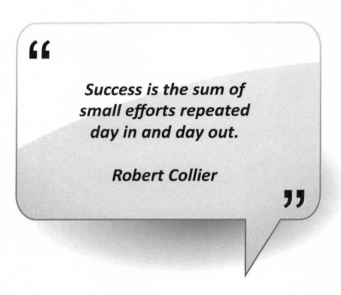

> **"**
>
> **Success is the sum of small efforts repeated day in and day out.**
>
> **Robert Collier**
>
> **"**

12.) Late Starts (8 Months To 18 Months):

If you begin late you will still use all the same rules, goals, and practices as I have outlined. Sit on the floor with your legs straddling the side of the potty and still face your little one. This one on one time and connection will help keep the child focused and zoned in while trying to eliminate. Use all the communicating, signing and verbal cues with older children. They may not physically connect to the verbal cue like infants do but they are captivated and intrigued and often find the cues funny. My friend's daughter, who was diaper trained, would laugh when I cued her and enjoyed making a strong connection with me over her bodily functions when she would come to my place. I would remove her diaper when she visited me and she actually began pooping in the potty while over at my apartment for the day!

The biggest thing with starting PTBT with toddlers is that there is no established routine and that they are busy playing. The best way to begin working with toddlers is to introduce using the potty directly after wake ups. Begin introducing potty opportunities at transition times, just as you do with infants. Once you've established a routine based on practicality and are communicating clearly, position the potty in the play area just as you do with the older babies who began training in infancy. Make sure your toddler knows that the potty chair is not a toy. If you see your child showing signs of needing to poop, no matter where they are, *bring the potty to them*. With late starts I really encourage this attitude because many will not want to stop what they are doing to try something unfamiliar. Once they get used to it you can take them to the potty when they need to go, but start out by *coming to them*.

Remember to use all the same tactics you do with infants, including setting a simple goal and slowly building from it. All communication goes a very long way as do the rules, consistency and positive feedback.

13.) Diet:

Remember these are little humans we are dealing with and just like adults a healthy diet, exercise and plenty of water will make for more regular elimination. All of our normal body functions experience change when we eat crappy food, travel, stay somewhere unfamiliar, or get sick. If our general health is failing one of the first signs of sickness is our stools and urine or lack thereof. Keep all of this in mind when communicating with your little one and never hold it against them if they poop their pants at Grandma's house after eating two chocolate bars!

For maximum digestive benefits and regular elimination, do your best to breastfeed until your baby is *at least* one year old. Feed your baby whole foods, grains, vegetables and fruits. Make your own baby food instead of buying it off the shelf; it is very easy to do. Plenty of water is essential

and is the best option besides breast milk. Please avoid infant formula, fast food, prepackaged meals, soda pop and candy. These items have been shown to cause constipation, improper digestion, heartburn and varying other maladies.

Understanding diet and how our health affects our elimination will help you to be much more aware of why an accident may have occurred, and how to avoid them. A little more awareness is a common thread within PTBT Method; it makes sense to *really* think about what we do and why we do it. Only good can come from that!

PTBT Method Refresher-

- Start Early
- Create a Simple Goal
- Tune in to Your Baby
- Use a Strong Cue
- Sit Baby up to Eliminate
- Communicate and Praise
- Transfer Baby to Potty
- Be Prepared and Keep Clean
- Create a Routine based off Observation and Baby's Needs
- Follow the Rules:
  Be Consistent and Be Positive!
- It's Never too Late to Start
- Pay Attention to Diet:
  What *Goes in* Effects What *Comes Out*!

A Little History, a Touch of Conspiracy and a Dash of Science

A Little History:

Having a baby is nothing new. Humans have been reproducing since the beginning of our race. There have been so many generations and so many cultures throughout the course of time that it would be presumptuous and uneducated to claim all parents performed the same method of potty training their infants. As in every aspect of multicultural study, each culture and each generation have variability based on religion, job duties, family size and dynamic, stature, knowledge, support, health and geographical location. Ancient Japanese families introduced their infants to pottying differently than Arctic Eskimo culture and babies born on the fertile, warm soil of Jamaica.

The common thread that all parents throughout time have had is dealing with human waste. Without getting into the realm of what these different cultures actually did with their waste, I want to focus on the fact that parents in the great majority taught their infants to deposit their excrement in the same or similar fashion as all other members of the family. The overall understanding and basic need was to teach their young as soon as possible to eliminate in the acceptable manner within that culture. If a family eliminated into bed pans, buckets, outside in a hole or into a river, their babies were taught just the same. Potty awareness was most commonly understood by the mother through intuition and communication and through the means of holding their babies in position over the chosen "receptacle".

Families in the following countries/regions have and/or still do engage in some form of PTBT and awareness. This list was compiled by Ingrid Bauer the author of *Diaper Free, The Gentle Wisdom of Natural Infant Hygiene*. These locations are only the most commonly documented, it is safe to say that everywhere around the world and throughout time until 1962 children were regularly potty trained well before 2 years old.

Afghanistan	Himalayas	Senegal
Alaska (Inuit)	India	Sikkim
Algeria	Iran	Solomon Islands
Austria	Iraq	South Africa
Bangladesh	Jamaica	Sri Lanka
Belize	Japan	Singapore
Botswana	Kenya	Taiwan
Brazil	Korea	Tibet
Burma	Mali	Turkey
Cameroons	New Guinea	Uganda
Canada (First Nations)	Nigeria	US (First Nations)
China	Pakistan	Vietnam
Germany	Peru	West Africa
Ghana	Russia	And many more...

In the majority of cultures elimination awareness is and has been developed through a mother's basic understanding of her child's needs through close proximity. It is common for mothers to carry their infants in slings and wraps to keep them close while mothers perform their daily duties. Occasionally a little cloth may be placed in the sling around the babies bottom but more often than not the babies are naked and the mothers have no reason to worry about being soiled. When mothers and fathers tune into their infant they easily develop a keen understanding of the baby's needs. The infant communicates the need to eliminate with his/her mother while curled into the sling, the mother then simply removes the baby from the wrap, lets the baby do his/her business and then she places the baby back into the warm retreat next to mama's body.

Parents never had a reason to question whether their infants were ready to *learn* to defecate and urinate. The idea is common sense to many cultures, of course babies know *how to release* waste from their bodies, they just need their families to listen to them and to show them the appropriate place. To question a baby's "readiness" for elimination is like asking the baby if it knew *how* to eat or *how* to sleep. The infant's needs are for care and guidance to master the inherent and instinctual knowledge he/she is born with.

Western diapering techniques have varied throughout time with the use of available fabric wrapped around the babies bum in the Middle Ages up to Elizabethan times where infants were swaddled in a "buttock cloth". These were unsanitary times and for some babies their cloth was only changed every four days. With the Industrial Revolution came higher standards of cleanliness and new found contraptions for diapering like safety pins, rubber pants and specially designed pre-fold cloth as well as wool "soakers". Despite the levels of filth through time and the drastic societal changes taking place, babies were commonly out of their mess at 6 months old up to 1 year in age.

The buildup of cities and the idea of modern convenience has been the bane of an infant's natural potty progression. With a major shift in thought and medical society becoming the last word on anything and everything, women were taken out of the equation in many ways. There was virtually no guide or handbook on birthing, breastfeeding, and potty training because women didn't need it. They knew instinctually and intuitively how to be mothers. Most women were having their babies at home with the help of a midwife and other women. Experienced women passed on the "tricks of the trade" and helped to guide each other into the truly remarkable new phase of being a mother.

When doctors had the official say, the families followed. This movement brought children out of the home for birth, disregarded midwives and questioned breastfeeding. Hospitals had the control over everything that came natural to a woman and this left many feeling powerless. Men ruled science and within that came birthing, breastfeeding, potty training and all other aspects of child care. These common sense and very natural

experiences were studied and theories arose from a clinical perspective. Women and children have been struggling to regain their natural equilibrium ever since.

The real experts were the mothers, but without that guidance being encouraged and even allowed in some areas, women began to look to the medical industry to tell them how and what to do with their bodies and their brethren. This new instruction of mothers led to the idea that they needed to be liberated from the drudgery of child care. Mothers were told to put babies on a pot at about 2 months of age to begin their potty training. This methodology was created partly with the obvious awareness that infants had the capabilities required for PTBT. Unfortunately the other half of this documented training approach was to "free up" a mother's time and was *not created* with the parents intuition in mind. It was to enforce a strict and regimented schedule of elimination for infants.

The level of sensitivity for parenting a potty training youngster swung back and forth from the 1800's until now. In 1932 the U.S. government published a guide entitled *"Infant Care."* The government encouraged the age old practice of starting babies eliminating into receptacles from birth and finishing with potty training at 6 to 8 months old. The scary and sadly missing element is that these guides were written by men and based off of theories with no connection to the *experience* of raising a child. The unspoken and undefined connection between a mother and baby was not referred to or comprehended and instead a frighteningly cold, clinical and cruel treatment was encouraged. The manual instructed mothers to, *"...insert a stick of soap into the baby's rectum or to stimulate their bottoms with the cold rim of a soap dish to induce a bowel movement."*

This "technique" had nothing to do with PTBT! The natural, loving bond that develops from understanding the needs of another human being was completely annihilated and strict time schedules were employed instead. Mothers were also told to empty the baby's bowels, *"twice daily, after the morning and evening bath, not varying the time by as much as five minutes."* The human being is not a machine no matter how much we organize and define our organs. With humanity comes variability and with that we have the power to grow and to change.

The habit of Western culture to take the living, intuitive, unexplainable element of life out of everything we do and replace it with a stagnant, forced, defined, linear program is the biggest tragedy of all. Countless families have been stripped of the ancient knowledge of connection and communication with their children. Many children have suffered from such a calculating and cold approach to child rearing, this is definitely the reason for the pendulum swing that brought doctors like Benjamin Spock to promote and very "child centered" approach to toilet training.

Little Bits of
Encouragement

*When we act with love
and think with kindness,
we are doing our best
and it is enough.*

I applaud Dr. Spock for trying to bring compassion back into child rearing with his book, *The Pocket Book of Baby and Child Care*, which was published in 1946. However with a lack of knowledge about the real power of PTBT awareness, he began his approach by encouraging parents to *wait* for potty training until their baby was 7 to 9 months old. I am sure that his intention was to veer families away from cruel parenting especially around potty training and him confusing the early starting time as a direct link to coercive methods was an honest, although a very unfortunate, mistake. With a mother's *real experience* out of the picture for over a hundred years there wasn't much authentic knowledge to go off of.

Even with parents waiting until 9 months to begin communicating with their babies about elimination, studies concurred in 1957 that 90 percent of babies were still out of diapers by 18 months. The question of the times wasn't if babies could do it, it was *how* parents dealt with teaching and assisting elimination needs. It was confusing times for women with a barrage of modern conveniences at their disposal and a major disconnect with their bodies through medical control. Washing machines, canned and pre-packaged foods were the acceptable signs of an advancing culture. The development of infant formula and the encouragement of a mother to use it instead of wasting time breastfeeding was popular and breastfeeding hit an all time low in the 1960's. The formula industry claimed that it was just as good as breast milk if not better and that "liberated" women needn't spend their time nursing infants. It was a brilliant marketing tool that fit the movement of a society at the right time. No other culture in the world has ever shown such a lack of respect for the brilliance of breast milk, no other culture could have been able to afford it.

A Touch of Conspiracy:

With breastfeeding waning and later starting times for potty training becoming the norm, families were systematically isolated. Mothers and babies were spending less and less time together and this made it very difficult to tap into the instincts and intuition required for true connection. The movement of Western society towards progress by the means of choking out intimacy and encouraging total independence paved the way for a proverbial "diaper revolution".

The model of diaper training that we currently follow in the United States was established in 1961 when Proctor and Gamble created Pampers, the first disposable diapers. The company hired a pediatrician by the name of T. Berry Brazelton to be their spokesperson. Brazelton conducted research which was highly lacking in any scientific integrity and reported his findings. He proclaimed that children who are potty trained too early tend to suffer emotionally and psychologically in later years. That potty training too early is hard on the psyche. He then suggested that parents wait until the child grows and can verbalize to the parents when they are ready for potty training. Like Dr. Spock, he wrongly tied early potty awareness to coercive and stringent parenting methods and then took his ideas one step further and tacked on almost a *year and a half* to Spock's suggested starting time!

The conspiracy factor is that despite the genuine concern for a child's mental and emotional health that Brazelton spoke of, the starting age for potty training he suggested was hugely exaggerated. He became an infomercial star explaining his "child-centered" approach to potty training. He encouraged parents to wait for all the "signs" that a child was emotionally, physically, and mentally ready to eliminate out of a diaper. Dr. Brazelton instructed caretakers that it was important for the child to initiate the process and to back off whenever the child decided he/she was bored or didn't want to use the potty anymore. The *only way* a family could maintain the amount of effort, time, and human waste management required for 2 to 3 years in diapers was to buy into the new wave of disposables. Families would not have been able to keep their kids in diapers that long using cloth; the work load would have been tremendous. Essentially the only pathway to allowing kids the "appropriate amount of time before potty training" was to use these new, convenient, amazing, oh so easy-breezy Pampers!! It worked and the disposable diaper industry took off with a vengeance.

Brazeltons belief was also to, once again, liberate mothers from the drudgery of dealing with their baby's waste by conveniently covering the children up and ignoring their needs until the child was old enough to ask to use the toilet. With all that *time saved* women could concentrate on more important tasks other than worrying about elimination. Despite Brazelton's certainty his research was splotchy and considered to actually prove the opposite of what he was touting as the head of the Pampers Institute and in numerous marketing ads. In his study published in, *Pediatrics* in 1962 he reported that 1/3 of children who potty trained *before* 2 years old were still wetting the bed at 3 ½ years old. Within this study that left the remaining 2/3s of 3 ½ year old bed wetter's not starting potty training until *after* 2 years old. Obviously there are benefits to early potty training from this evidence.

Dr. T. Berry Brazelton also concluded, as part of the same study, that of the children still wetting the bed after 5 years old, 87.5 percent had begun potty training at 2 years old or older. Only 12.5 percent of children who had this lasting problem of bed wetting at 5 years old began early training before 2 years of age. Brazelton effectively twisted his research around and made a point to only report the percentages related to early potty training so as to paint a negative picture. The research was based on one study with a highly marginalized group and had zero historical evidence, especially from that of other cultures.

Unfortunately most pediatricians followed suit and the idea was widely accepted by the American public. Parents thought they were helping their children and coupled with the idea of modern convenience, ease and the baby staying "clean and dry" in their diapers, the popularity of disposable's grew quickly. The diaper industry has skyrocketed and has been a stabilized multibillion dollar industry for years. Proctor and Gamble and other corporations have been spreading their packaged convenience to foreign countries that have been completely oblivious to this need of diapers. In effect, convincing communities through intensive advertising campaigns to upgrade into a more "civilized and modern" approach to toilet training. The sad part is that when elimination awareness and intuitive techniques are ignored within traditional cultures the majority of families have difficult, frustrating and expensive experiences with diaper training. Not to mention the huge environmental impact disposable diapers have on communities not set up to deal with exorbitant amounts of non-biodegradable plastic wrapped around raw sewage.

Many well-meaning pediatricians continue to applaud parents for waiting until their children initiate toilet use as they believe it shows a sign of respect for the child's body, even if their body was kept hidden in diapers for several years. A Pampers ad claims,

"Don't rush your toddler into toilet training or let anyone else tell you it's time! It's got to be his choice!"

Pampers is "lovingly" there to help parents deal with these added years of toilet training by offering a *size six* disposable. More pediatricians are beginning to suggest parents wait until their children are 4 or 5 years old to begin potty training, this way parents can bypass the struggle of the "terrible twos" and "terrible threes" stages. Diapers are showing up on the market in extra large and jumbo sizes to accommodate the thousands of older children running around in *pull-ups* and still needing elimination support.

A Dash of Science:

When we examine the human body using a common sense approach we can easily see that a human knows innately how to breathe, sleep, eat and eliminate because without those four elements we would soon die. Our bodies take time to develop biologically and for our systems to mature, yet our basic life sustaining functions are active from birth. Infants communicate their need to be fed just the same as their need to eliminate. We have been trained as an advanced society, in the past sixty years, to ignore the signs for elimination. We have been told these signs do not exist therefore we act as if elimination communication is not happening. When a babies needs are ignored or responded to negatively he/she will shut down into a state of survival, they will naturally take the path of least resistance.

Developing *full control* over the bladder and bowels comes with practice, encouragement and natural development as does learning to balance, sitting up, walking and talking. However, possessing an instinctual *knowing* is another story. To positively reinforce and respond to a baby's innate understanding of his/her self we assist in the ability to learn control over his/her own body. The more awareness we possess of our physical and psychological selves the more power we have to develop our potential.

The concept of cueing babies is as old as PTBT itself and is a very effective means of encouraging self awareness and developmental growth. Every culture has a variance on the cue being used but in countries all over the world most mothers' use a "sssss" sound to stimulate or signal a *release*. This makes sense as that is the sound of running water, and is associated with a feeling of relaxing the body. Parents cue their babies as they are eliminating. Very quickly an infant associates *this sound, this cue, this communication* with the physical act of eliminating. Once a baby becomes connected to the cue a parent will hold the baby over a receptacle and make the cue noise, the baby will instantly release his/her sphincter muscles.

In the first infant potty training book I read connecting to a cue through instinct was associated with the physical response we have when watching a balloon pop. This "balloon effect" is realizing that once we have heard the sound or cue of the balloon popping we will instinctually prepare our bodies for this cue again by huddling up, closing our eyes and scrunching up our faces. This has been proven in studies by a demonstrator holding a balloon and then slowly taking a sharp pin to the surface of the balloon. Long before there is a sound the entire group of volunteers are instinctually preparing for the noise! Now that the balloon pop has been established, we will react with apprehension and preparation if we think we are about to hear that sound. The physical connection from the balloon effect and PTBT cueing is obvious; we develop instinctual responses to our environments.

The difference between the two is that cueing takes it up a notch with elimination occurring *after* the instinctual response. This is very important to understand, when the cue has been established through deep connection and awareness a baby will release his/her sphincter muscles every time he/she hears the cue, however, this does not mean that feces and urine will come out every time! This is not a magic trick and if a baby does not have to eliminate you cannot make him/her automatically pee or poop because of the cue sound. It is a *message* to the body, an *invitation* to relax and release and a very deep level of communication. Using a cue is a powerful way to communicate but if a parent is completely disconnected with their babies natural potty rhythms and cycles and still expects constant results both parent and child will struggle. John Rosemond, a well known author and family therapist, pointed out that potty training early will not cause horrific psychological and physical effects as the Pampers Institute had exclaimed, but parents who use harsh criticism and forceful training approaches create that.

We have seen through history that it has been scientifically proven that children have the ability and the know how to potty train far earlier than currently suggested. Less than a century ago children in Europe and North America were commonly out of diapers anywhere from a few weeks old to one year. Before disposable diapers were available in 1961, 90 percent of children were fully finished with potty training by 2 ½ years old, by 1998 a little under 40 years later only 22 percent of children were potty trained by 2 ½. Currently in numerous countries around the world and throughout history, a baby's readiness is known from birth. Families who are introduced to the western idea of readiness and waiting for the child are appalled, confused and disgusted at such an act that keeps children in filth for years on end.

Dr. Barton Schmitt wrote an article published in *Contemporary Pediatrics*,

"To keep toilet training in perspective, remember that *more than 50%* of children around the world are toilet trained at about 1 year in age."

Why do western raised children, specifically those of North America, fall so far behind in their physical development? Why do children all over the world complete potty training far earlier than children in the United States? The only answer is that our culture does not actively practice what every other culture knows to be true. This fact proves the safety, viability, and reality of elimination communication and PTBT. Parents in the United States wanted to do the right thing for our children but we soldiered on with ever more time saving inventions. Most parents forgot or were never told how early children could really connect with their bodies and we began keeping our toddlers in diapers long after they were "ready" merely for convenience sake. Unfortunately it was an *assumed* convenience at a high cost.

Author Ingrid Bauer stated,

"On the days when I felt like I was the only one in the world that was doing Natural Infant Hygiene with her baby, it felt good to be reminded that I was not alone. I was in the good company of mothers from all over the world."

It is important to remember that as we feel lost in a sea of modern advances and technology, practicing PTBT Method ties us together with more women and more history than we could ever imagine. I like that feeling.

> **"**
>
> *Courage doesn't always roar. Sometimes courage is the quiet voice at the end of the day saying, I will try again tomorrow.*
>
> **Mary Anne Radmacher**
> **"**

Western parents are currently in the midst of an epidemic of potty "untrained" children. Many are confused and angry at the fact that their children experience bed wetting late into elementary school years and show numerous fears around pooping. A vast number of children suffer from constipation and incontinence. Dr. William Sears, a famous pediatrician, endorses the use of early potty training and has witnessed a surge of families interested in the practice due to negative experience from the "readiness approach". It seems that our culture is beginning to recognize the wrong path that we have been traveling when it comes to our infant's awareness. More and more pediatricians are researching the negative physical effects of long term diaper use. They are also looking into other societies and into history for increased knowledge. No sense in reinventing the wheel, right?

In October 2005 Canadian National Radio broadcast Ingrid Bauer author of, *Diaper Free The Gentle Wisdom of Natural Infant Hygiene*, a book I highly recommend everyone to read. She was interviewed along with Dr. T. Brazelton; Ingrid mentioned in her book that she was delighted to hear words like "lovely", "wonderful" and "convincing" coming from Brazelton's mouth when discussing elimination communication. During the interview Brazelton expressed his wish that,

"...more women could be free enough to do it that way" (using elimination communication), and "...it would be wonderful if they did." He stated that his methodology was "...an adaptation to the way we live."

He stated he believed it was too difficult to reproduce the use of ancient reliable methods in our society due to so many women needing to be in the workforce.

I was moved when I read of this interview and of the connective tissue between Ingrid Bauer and Dr. Brazelton. I feel PTBT Method may just be the perfect approach to bridging this theoretical gap. Roxana and I naturally veered off from some of elimination communication's classic standards. We created a method that incorporated all of the current struggles of an advanced and fast paced society. Many of those struggles being single parent homes, working fulltime and feeling disconnected from our responsibility as mothers. PTBT Method manifested as a link between drastically different lifestyles and perspectives.

As an example, my choice to use a potty chair from the beginning instead of *holding* Roxana over a receptacle saved my knees and my back from all the bending over and waiting for elimination to occur. I used the potty chair time also for eye contact and face to face connection. With the busy lifestyle of a single parent it was hard to get down with Roxana for lots of one on one time. Creating a pleasing, comfortable and connective experience during her elimination was a benefit to both of us. I believe the PTBT Method is accessible to all parents living in our fast paced western culture. I hope that thousands of years of practical experience and loving parenting outweighs the desire to move so fast we leave our children far behind. As Ingrid Bauer so beautifully put it, the choice to practice (elimination communication) is,

"…in essence a political, social, environmental, and economic act, as well as a deeply personal one."

Save Some Money, Save Some Earth, Save Some Babies, Save Some Time

Save Some Money:

With an *Ambulatory Pediatrics* article in 2001 reporting that the average potty training age rose to 35 months for girls and 39 months for boys we are looking at roughly three years of buying diapers. This has been estimated to equal up to 9,000 diapers per child at a cost of $3,000 to $6,000 depending on the brands of diapers used. Keep in mind this does not include the cost of wipes, diaper rash ointments, powders, lotions, changing table, diaper pails, wipe warmers, diaper bags and training books/videos, etc. All of the extras that come with diaper training add up to an estimated additional $1,500 over the child's diaper wearing years. That is $4,500 at a *minimum* for a 3 year old child.

Many families continue to rack up the bill with children training late into their 3rd year as well as continuing diaper use into the 4th and 5th year. Adding to the already staggering costs of disposable diapers are the children who suffer for years from the trained disconnect to their elimination cycles. A record amount of children in their 5th, 6th and 7th years still request diapers to be put on them in order to feel comfortable pooping, as this is how they were trained. We have all seen the many commercials for the big kid pull ups, weighing in at a size 6. It has become very common for diaper trained children to suffer from incontinence and therefore have steady accidents at night requiring the need for disposable diaper use into the later years of grade school.

An alternative to disposables are cloth diapers which will save some money and typically children will potty train much sooner. Cloth diapers still pack a cost for natural resources and our pocketbooks when children train at 3 years old. Parents can purchase two dozen good quality cloth diapers for under $75 also covers and liners adding up to $300 or more. Factoring in the cleaning products, water and energy costs for three years the bill could come to $800 to $1,000. Totaled up, families look at significantly lower costs than disposable diapers but still require extra time and clean up than letting babies eliminate straight into a potty. The cost of a diaper service for three years is estimated to be over $2,000 and although it is convenient for the family dirty diapers require 12 washes and the use of chemicals to sterilize and balance the PH of the diapers. The extensive *resource* cost for a diaper service can be a major turn off.

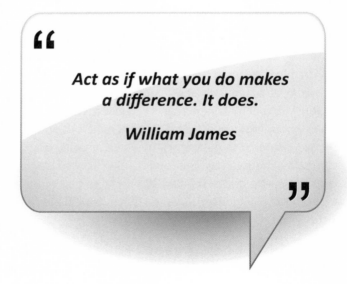

Act as if what you do makes a difference. It does.

William James

When Roxana wore diapers it was pretty common for the poop to slosh up the back and out the sides to mortally stain her onesies. I had to toss several outfits because they were so badly stained. I know these poop "blow outs" are a common occurrence for many families and child care workers. Allowing a baby to release feces in the proper receptacle saves not only diapers but clothes that could be potentially recycled through thrift store donations. Companies rope us in with the ever enchanting idea of *convenience* but at a high financial cost to the unaware consumer. Thousands of dollars can be saved by tapping into the PTBT Method. I am sure we all could find better ways to invest our hard earned money!

Save Some Earth:

From manufacture to landfill, disposable diapers have a major impact on our environment. The creation process of single use diapers is extreme and requires enormous amounts of natural resources. Studies show that over one billion trees per year go into diapers, tons of water and a bevy of chemicals. Factor in a ½ pint of crude oil *per each* disposable diaper produced and you have a major amount of petroleum product being consumed. Manufacturing disposables emits highly toxic dioxin and furans into our environment. Dioxin has been found to be a carcinogen which we all know causes cancer, nerve damage and many more maladies.

According to the research of Linda Sonna, PH.D., the author of *Early Start Potty Training*, the European based Greenpeace found organotins, a type of dioxin, in Proctor and Gambles Pampers and Pampers Baby Dry Mini and in the Fixies Ultra Dry disposable diapers. These toxic chemicals and compounds are often used in the highly coveted super absorbent gel. The negative effects of organotins have inclined Greenpeace to request for the ban of *all organotins in all products worldwide*. These are the same chemicals linked to toxic shock syndrome in women from tampon use, immune system damage and the inhibition of the tumor killing ability of a body's natural killer cells.

According to an article in the New York Times, *22 billion* single use disposable diapers are thrown into landfills each year. That many diapers stretched out make about 100 trips around the world. Those billions of diapers add up to a frightening 1/3 of the nonbiodegradable trash in our nation's dumps. Keeping with the previously discussed average potty training age of roughly 3 years old, *each child* contributes nearly *3 tons* of used diapers

to the landfills by the time they are potty trained. "Disposable" diapers do not go away they will still be sitting in landfills many generations after the babies who wore them.

Environmental Overload

½ pint of crude oil per each diaper

22 billion disposable diapers per year thrown into landfills

Each child adds 3 tons to the waste

Plastic from diapers may take more than 500 years to disintegrate

Toxic chemicals used in disposables seep into the Earth, air and water supply

In a study called the "*Human Footprint*" done by National Geographic and 20/20 it was estimated that it would take 500 years for disposable diapers to breakdown, however, no one is sure what the real life expectancy of plastic is. 500 years could be small change compared to how long it will really take for the diaper to truly be "disposed" of. During this time toxins seep from the diaper into the Earth poisoning soil and water sources. Not to mention the fatal impact filthy toxic diapers have on the unsuspecting wildlife who mistakenly takes a bite out of hunger.

if this reality weren't bad enough there is another element to consider. When we throw away diapers we chuck them out filled with untreated human waste. It is actually illegal to dispose of untreated waste yet we get away with it by wrapping up the mess in little plastic time bombs. This leads to tons of raw sewage leaking into our ground water, a devastating and completely irresponsible act on our part. With our population growing at an unprecedented rate it is urgent that we protect our water supplies. Becoming more responsible with how and where we deposit human waste is vital to the survival of future generations.

Save Some Babies:

External physical damage

At one point as I diapered Roxana, I realized that I was very concerned about money and that worry manifested in my care for her. There were times, before I recognized my behavior, that I chose to keep a used diaper on her because she had only peed once and once wasn't enough! I felt that if the diaper companies were right the urine was magically "whisked away from her body" therefore I could keep her in them longer to maximize their "science". I had subconsciously accepted through media programming that it was wasting too many diapers and essentially too much money if Roxana only urinated in them once. When I realized I had done this, it made me sick to my stomach and I immediately stopped.

Recently, at the park, I was pushing Roxana in the swing next to a little boy age 2. His mom turned to me and asked me if I had an extra diaper. I told her no, that I'd practiced PTBT Method and that my daughter had been potty trained for well over a year. She was shocked and said she wished she'd done something like that. Her predicament was that she had carried her son down a very big hill which was a good journey with hundreds of steep steps to get to the park. Her son had pooped on the way down the stairs. She had come all that way and he really wanted to swing so she didn't have the heart to turn back around and go back up the hill without her child getting a little fun. So she took him to the bathroom, rinsed the disposable diaper off with water and put it back on him. I was mortified. I knew she was a new mom and young and didn't need me making her feel bad about what she was doing, she needed support. I suggested she remove the diaper and to let him go without it for a bit before they headed back up to the car. She was too scared to try. This loving mother and her son were so convinced of the dire need for diapers that a filthy, feces infested diaper was a better alternative than a bare bottom.

It made me worry that if I had chosen to prolong my daughters contact to urine to save money, with my awareness and on such a small scale, what do other parents do? If this young mother was trying her best to care for her child but was thoroughly convinced by marketing that she had no alternative but to use a filthy diaper, how many more caretakers do the same thing? How long do some parents let their babies soak in their own urine or worse, how long before they notice that their child has a diaper full of poop? This reality was disturbing and it is obviously a real issue.

Diaper rash is so common place these days I had never really stopped to think about what it is. Essentially diaper rash is feces and urine eating away the layers of a baby's skin. Disgusting! It's insane that we would create an environment and willingly disregard their flesh. Even if babies are changed often there is always the chance that poop gets hidden in their folds, especially for chubbier little ones. These areas are breeding grounds for diaper wounds. Why sell so many creams and lotions to help remedy the after effects if children weren't suffering from this awful torture?

Parents and child care workers believe what the disposable diaper companies' tell us, that our children are "staying clean and dry because the super absorbent pads whisk away the mess!" The *reality* is that the toxic chemicals used to create super absorbency diapers suck up the urine and hold it flush up against the baby's skin. Children do not stay "clean" by any stretch of the imagination. Sodium polyacrylate, another chemical associated with toxic shock syndrome that was banned from tampons is found in the super absorbent gel in diapers. It is likely this substance is responsible for severe diaper rash as well as perineal tissue damage.

Diaper rash has become a very standard and excepted part of infancy. Obviously "diaper rash" is directly connected to the "diaper". The diaper is the sole cause of this common rash that can range from mild red bumps and irritation to open puss filled wounds. Wearing diapers creates a warm, moist environment which is a bacterial wet dream. Ammonia which is present in all urine burns skin. Extended burning of skin via ammonia can lead to permanent scarring and tissue death called necrosis.

With the combination of feces and urine burning skin, abrasive constant rubbing of plastic and/or bleached fabric and direct contact with a bevy of chemical and unnatural materials we create a wonderland for viral, bacterial and fungal infections. The chances of toddlers contracting *E. coli* which is present in feces are greatly increased. The microscopic bacteria enter the blood stream through tiny wounds in the skin and cause diarrhea, cramps and severe abdominal pain. The Centers for Disease Control and Prevention stated that,

"...toddlers, who are not toilet trained, as well as family members and playmates, are at high risk of becoming infected."

Chemical exposure increases respiratory issues in children and little boys may experience fertility damage from increased heat on their scrotum.

Disposable diapers have not been around long enough for us to have clear studies on the effects of the chemicals used. Also as the "absorbency science" has gotten more advanced we have introduced countless toxins into newer diapers. Many of the additives have not been thoroughly tested and evaluated for long term effects. We all see the short term effects riddling our children with pain and discomfort. As parents and child care workers it is our responsibility to protect the physical health of children's skin.

Little Bits of Encouragement

Remember, we try to do the best we can with the knowledge we have. Guilt about what we did not know is painful and unnecessary.

Can you even imagine having your entire butt and genitals crammed in a hot, stuffy, plastic contraption 24 hours a day!? Then think about the fact that your diaper would usually contain some amount of urine and you were subject to feces being squished all over your goods. Yuck! Seriously, when we stop to think about it, diapering isn't a safe practice and it just doesn't make very much sense.

Physiological problems/Internal physical damage

Diapering our babies causes damage on the outside of the body as well as the inside of the body. A study done by E. Bakker in 2001 and was reported in the *Scandinavian Journal of Urology and Nephrology* concluded that *all* of the children within his study, that had bladder problems at age 11 *all* began potty training *after* 2 years old. Delayed potty training has been associated with increased bladder infections, frequent urination, an unstable bladder and bed wetting. Another study done and published in 2000 entitled, *"Changes in the Toilet Training of Children During the Last Sixty Years: The Cause of an Increase in Lower Urinary Tract Dysfunction?"* concluded that the answer to this question was a solid YES. Increased bed wetting has become quite common in our modern society with a number of diapering options available to assist our elementary school aged children with overnight visits, as we see on the commercials. The fact that so many children suffer from incontinence is alarming and is not a "normal" part of growing up. We, as parents and guardians of children, have to realize our beliefs about elimination are generating negative experiences for kids.

Digestion issues often occur due to the diapers being too tight around the baby's belly. Many parents have found that by removing the diaper and responding to their infant's elimination needs they have witnessed better digestion, a decrease in constipation and even diminished colicky behavior. Allowing babies to sit on the potty and release with the flow of gravity increases strength in the pelvic floor and is helpful to the digestive tract. The tight band around a baby's belly directly affects their ability to eliminate effectively. To bring this idea to a level we can more identify with; on a recent Dr. Oz episode he had a segment entitled, *Fashion Trends that Can Cause Health Dangers*. He stated,

"Tight jeans can cause your intestines to become restricted, which can lead to constipation and digestive issues."

He also showed how cutting off the top of our stomach with such steady pressure causes a back up in our bowels. His trick to determine whether we wear our jeans too tight was to place a tube of lipstick between the waistband of your jeans and your waist. If your lipstick won't fit, your jeans are too tight. I can tell you right now it is very unlikely that any baby wearing a disposable diaper would be able to fit a tube of lipstick between his/her body and the diaper. We tend to pull them tightly across the belly so as to reduce the chance of a "blow out" happening and feces escaping. Applied pressure on the intestines is very dangerous, it affects adults and we can all attest to that. The truth is that babies can suffer far more damage because their organs and systems are still developing.

Psychological problems

A baby's natural instinct is to pee and poop in the open, not all crammed into a diaper. A parent will see this situation a lot in infancy, when as soon as the diaper is removed the baby instantly pees or poops. Infants know instinctually that this is the way to eliminate but we train them to stop doing what is natural and to release into their diapers. We begin at birth to teach our infants to ignore their natural human-animal instincts, a very tragic practice in my opinion.

A disconnect of mind and body created through extended diaper training is one of the longest lasting and more subtle traumas. We teach them to disconnect from their intuition and to ignore all of the subtle signs our bodies offer our minds as a means of communication. A body wants to live in harmony with itself. The brain and body send information constantly to each other to establish understanding and flow. When we teach our children to ignore these vitally important feelings and inner knowledge we strip them of an enormous power.

We teach our children, without intent, to feel mentally separate from their physical body, to feel ashamed and embarrassed by sudden explosions of bodily waste. If we are not connected to our physical processes and do not live in acceptance and honor them, then our only other choice is to view them as negative. We hide from our body and its filthy habits of elimination. The psychological implications from this type of anti-connection training can manifest in thousands of ways, from basic insecurity to extreme fear of eliminating in public. Many adults in our current, advanced society have such an intense anxiety about eliminating in public they will go through great lengths to hold in their waste or will not leave home unless they are certain they will not have to poop while out. Running from our elimination cycles is a losing battle, without a properly functioning digestive and filter system we get sick and die.

The time spent in diapers can cause tremendous confusion about the purpose of genitals. Our genitals have two very important and very different roles. Often times parents and caretakers are so scared of the sexual application of human genitalia that they create a negative "no zone" for the region altogether. Elimination gets turned into a dirty thing coming from a bad place. Having negative thoughts about our bodies is not a healthy practice. Turning natural development and function into a bad, evil or disgusting experience can manifest into extreme psychosis. Negative self image and a negative sexual perspective of yourself and the sex act in general can lead to increased susceptibility to molestation, rape and abuse in all forms.

It is so funny and well, disgusting, but this situation happens all the time; A group of adults standing around talking, maybe at a barbeque or family event. There is light discussion about the kids and then someone invariably says,

"Oh, it looks like little Johnny is taking a dump."

All the adults look and laugh because it is obvious by the little tykes red face that he is pooping and filling up his diaper. I have been a part of this dynamic countless times and did not give it a second thought until I became educated about our children's abilities. Now when I experience this, I say,

"Whoa, let's get him on the potty!"

Please, parents and caretakers, I implore you...when you see that your or someone else's child has to poop, especially when they are of walking age, do not just stand and watch! Take them to the bathroom and let them unload! It just makes more sense in so many ways. Don't we all agree that it is important to teach our children where poop really needs to go? At some point they will be taught, so the earlier the better.

These experiences for children can be traumatizing. From 2 years old children are fully aware. The embarrassment kids feel when they are laid down by another person who has to mop up the child's stinky poop can really be hard to get over. Especially due to the comments parents and others make about the smell or size of the fecal mess. All of these comments are absorbed by our children. They will pack away those little pellets of shame right into their psyche. They may never say a word about it but those feelings will manifest in other ways. People can be cruel about having to clean up that kind of mess, changing diapers doesn't really make anyone happy.

If we reduced the need and the length of time for these all around uncomfortable situations we may be able to offer some protection and positive guidance for our children. The PTBT Method balances the practical reality of our modern lives with teaching and showing self acceptance, intuitive and instinctual awareness, and healthy physical and psychological development. It is a gift that we have the power to give.

Save Time:

If you are feeling like there is no way you can practice PTBT Method because it would take up too much time, keep this in mind. A child potty trained at roughly 3 years old is estimated to have experienced up to 9,000 diaper changes in their life. It takes time to put diapers on your babies and to take them off. It takes time to wipe them, powder them and apply ointment. It takes time to heal diaper rash wounds; it takes time to drive to the store for more wipes, diapers and ointments. It takes time to take out the garbage from the nursery; it takes time to put away the new diapers and accoutrements.

It takes time to work to get more money to support all the diapering costs, it takes time to do the additional laundry and stain removal for damaged clothes. It takes time to pack and unpack diapering needs for outings; it takes time for a toddler to unlearn his/her diaper training; it takes even more time to re-teach him/her how to use the potty. Many American families have children in diapers at 4 years old, and a number of children are experiencing bladder issues and have accidents at night causing children ages 5, 6 and 7 years old to wear nighttime diapers. Think about all the time that takes.

Roxana has had an amazing journey with PTBT Method. Eliminating is so second nature at nearly 3 years old, and has been for so long, that we save tons of time and more importantly worry. Our outings are fun and I am excited because I have no need to stress about her very basic human elimination functions. Roxana can relax too, she is not worried about it, she tells me when she's got to go and I ask her periodically to cover our bases. She doesn't feel scared, ashamed, uncomfortable or stressed. From 1 ½ years old she's experienced her life full of so many new wonders. We've been able to fly comfortably, take long car trips, go swimming, spend the whole day out at the beach, parks, stores, and events and we do not have to waste time worrying about diapers or accidents. Roxana does not spend her hours with any more concern about her needing to eliminate than she does about her need to sleep or eat. We deal with her physical needs and mine as they come, with a little preparation and awareness we have been limitless. She was given the opportunity to become in tune with the very rote needs of humanity at the appropriate time... the very beginning of her life.

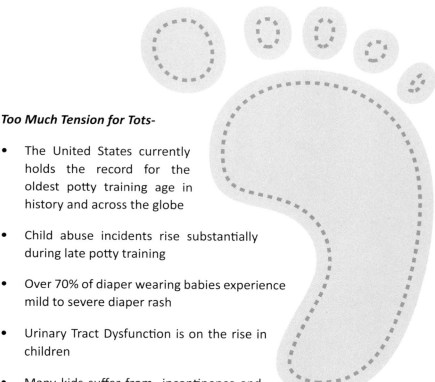

Too Much Tension for Tots-

- The United States currently holds the record for the oldest potty training age in history and across the globe

- Child abuse incidents rise substantially during late potty training

- Over 70% of diaper wearing babies experience mild to severe diaper rash

- Urinary Tract Dysfunction is on the rise in children

- Many kids suffer from incontinence and bed-wetting through grade school

- Shame and embarrassment are feelings associated with late potty training

- Babies experience a disconnect to their bodies and as they grow have a very difficult time reconnecting to their bodily functions

My Theories on Parental Sanity, Child Abuse, Child Molestation and Education

This chapter is bound to stir up a bit of activity! My intention is not to be controversial; it is not to act as if I have it all figured out or place blame. I've entitled this section, *my theories*, because that is exactly what they are. I hope by being painfully honest, by sharing my thoughts and ideas that they may open some eyes. This may get some people thinking about their behavior and that they have the power to change it. My purpose is awareness.

I love my daughter more than anything. I love children, in all their shapes and sizes and developmental stages. I will always provide a safe and loving environment for any children in my care. I wish that I could guarantee this fundamental care for all children. I know that many of you feel the same way. It is my hope, from the deep recesses of my heart and knowledge of my experience, that what I share provokes positive change. I hope that I may offer assistance in any way I can to protect our children.

Parental Sanity:

The dramatic reality within child abuse and sexual abuse cases is that most of the offenders experienced these horrors as children as well. It is predominately *a cycle* of pain and brutality. As parents, I believe the more honest we are about our struggles and strife, the more safety we will find with our feelings and as a direct result the more safe our children will be. I have seen over and over again, a major separation between good parents and the monster parents we see on the news. The devastating effects of what some people do drive the majority of parents into a frenzy of "us vs. them." Most horrific crimes generate this kind of behavior. I have found myself after having my daughter, very matter of factly, saying that the man on the news who had just killed his 3 year old daughter and his wife, should be shot in the head. Boom... done with that bastard.

I have found my protective feelings for my daughter creating a very distinct boundary and anyone who crosses it deserves and has asked for, certain death. But what are the *realities* of these situations? No story is black and white. Very, very few stories of violence and abuse, of rape and theft, happen just because someone was born a monster.

I had an interesting experience last year when I went out of state with my daughter for a friend's wedding. My girlfriend dropped us at the airport in my car and she asked if she could use it the next day to pick up a visiting friend from New York. Of course I said sure, as she had done me a favor so I would do her one. She just lived down the street from me and we live in a "safe" neighborhood. The next day I get a call from her in a completely frantic state. My car was gone! She had locked it up the night before and now it had vanished.

I was taking a tiny vacation from all the work and the stress of being a single mom and working full time. I had a wedding to attend and I wanted to have a relaxed time. This was not a good start. The reality of my circumstances was that I was the sole provider, I had a little girl about 14 months old and I had to work full time to keep everything together. It was definitely a requirement for my job that I have a car which was reliable and could carry several hundred pounds of weight consistently. Also my car was paid for which was an enormously important aspect. Now it was gone.

I battled my feelings for the weekend trip and tried to stay positive. When we got back home I opened the door to my apartment and I was hit very hard in the face with a blast of gas! My apartment was filled with gas. It poured into the hallway from my leaking water heater. I had left all of my windows open while gone but my apartment was still so thick with gas fumes that my friend and I immediately got headaches and felt very sick. I turned it off, called the manager and went down the street to spend the night elsewhere. I laughed and cried that night because what can you do when your car is stolen and it is currently your livelihood and then you come home to an apartment filled with gas?

A week later my car was found; it had been towed because it was in an undrivable condition. I was freaked out and nervously went to the towing lot. I was told I owed $174 for the tow and was given a bill. I had tears streaming down my face. I walked into the yard and found my car. It was stripped beyond anything I could have imagined. Tires gone, hood gone, engine gone, insides cut up. The steering wheel was gone, dashboard gone, everything. Roxana's car seat, her clothes, toys and shoes that had been in there were all gone. Even the little Mexican art angel my dad had given me that hung on the rearview mirror was gone; it had been ripped from the string that still dangled there. I was destroyed. I had only been able to afford liability insurance and I still had to pay for the tow. I had to walk away with a roughly $8,000 loss.

The reason I explain this story is because for a few days I stomped around the city with hatred burning in my heart. I was skeptical of everyone. Friends made comments about me learning my lesson, never lending my car out or anything else for that matter. It wouldn't have happened if I hadn't lent it to my girlfriend. There was blame, guilt, regret and fury flying around. I felt it was me against "them". But who the hell is "them" anyway?

One day as I walked down the street in a huff it occurred to me that I couldn't spend the rest of my life in fear and without trust. I know that even if "those" people are doing bad things they are doing it for a reason. Maybe another little child was riding around safe in Roxana's car seat. Maybe someone was holding my angel and feeling love because it was so beautiful and a protector. Maybe a family ate a year's worth of full hot meals because of the parts of my car that were sold. It was a tough economy; people had to do whatever they could to make it. It did not make it *ok*; it just made it *real*. This was just how life works, when people are hurt they often hurt back.

Wasn't I thankful and lucky that Roxana and I had been out of town that weekend and I wasn't home to light the candle that could have blown us up, or that I could have kissed her goodnight and never woke again to see her lovely face? Wasn't this some sort of ridiculous opportunity? An energetic exchange; my life and my daughter are saved from being gassed in our sleep at the bargain price of a car. You bet your sweet ass I'd pay with my car; I'd pay whatever I had to, to keep us safe and alive.

I overcame my anger and fear and I empathized with the stress that people were experiencing. I willingly let go of what I had lost and said out loud, "I hope that what I gave you helps you." I also thanked the universe for my daughter's life and my own and I moved on. I was able to get another vehicle that I am still making payments on, but I am healthy and so is my child. My heart is filled with love and not hatred. I trust people, and if a friend ever needed to borrow anything I would willingly oblige. Sacrifices happen all over the world, in every moment, in every breath we take. We have the choice to let it break us or to let it build us.

> **"**
>
> *Faith is taking the first step even when you don't see the whole staircase.*
>
> *Dr. Martin Luther King Jr.*
>
> **"**

This is important because it is a story of coming out of the *"us vs. them"* attitude and creating empathy for *them* therefore, strength within *us*. I feel that if parents could empathize more with what other parents go through, if we were honest about how difficult being a parent really is then we might save each other from our own hurtful potential.

Pretend there was a parent who was ashamed at his/her feelings of wanting to stifle the sound of his/her infant crying. This parent broke down often because he/she was so exhausted and felt like he/she was falling off the edge. If this parent had someone to talk to, someone to confide in maybe this could relieve the true stress and anger or resentment he/she felt towards the baby. Maybe, just maybe, that would be enough to take the cap off the bottle. Maybe enough steam would be released to bring that parent back down to a space that he/she could handle the daily frustrations without feeling likely to snap and hit the child.

It is not acceptable to talk about wanting to beat your children. Of course not! It sounds absolutely horrific. But if you are a parent and I mean a parent who truly takes care of your child, day in and day out, there are times when you want to throw them through a wall! It is the toughest job in the world and I am not just saying that. It is the most strenuous and requires, by far, the most patience of any job. There are times when the most calm, loving and nurturing mother feels she will pull her hair out from the roots if they do not step away for two minutes. There are nights that even the richest, most powerful people desperately want their baby to stop crying and they can understand why people suffocate their babies with pillows.

I know it is hard to read and probably makes you feel sick to your stomach but this is the *reality* and child abuse happens *all the time*. What can we do about it? I think the most important thing we can do is start being honest about how hard parenting is and honest about how far it can take you. I believe that if more parents felt there was a middle ground somewhere between being a perfect parent and being a monster, we might be able to keep some people from falling off the edge.

Imagine this, a good parent who is under a lot of stress and feels so guilty about his/her negative feelings toward his/her children the feelings stay bottled up which then creates even more pain. He/she can't tell anyone about how it feels because what would people think? The parent keeps trying to ignore the feelings everyday but the stress compiles and it is harder and harder. Late one night after a really tough day, that parent crosses over and hits his/her child to stop the little one from crying. The parent feels horrible and promises he/she will *never* do it again. The problem is that now a release has been found for the never ending buildup of stress and pain inside of his/her mind and heart. The cycle of abuse begins. The parent can never admit to what they did because the shame is too great. And now that the abuse has happened, the initial jump has taken place; the parent has found that he/she can "release" through hitting more readily than before.

If we create an outlet for this kind of stress, the unspeakable kind of feelings that parents feel, wouldn't that be a start at protecting our children?

My girlfriend Laura and I were lucky that we were both raising babies at similar times. Her daughter is nearly 8 months older than mine but close enough. Laura is happily married, her husband makes very good money and they have really everything they need and have access to most of what they want. Their daughter is very smart and creative and she is a handful. She just seems out of control sometimes, not like she is being bad out of control but just that she has so much energy she is going to burst. She is an intense little girl with intense feelings and emotions, the yang to the yin of her very mellow, easy going and supportive mother. Laura and I were opposite in our living situations but she and I both could identify with the struggles of raising a baby. Laura and I have always been close and very honest with each other but we found a new level of this in the first two years of our children's lives.

We created a sort of game. I don't remember when it started or who said something first but we created a space of utter honesty to the point of complete absurdity. We talked about everything going on in our lives and all the wonderful things we experienced being new mothers, but there was also the very heavy reality that it was tough. Even given our totally different lifestyles, it was difficult to be steady every day and every night, over and over and over again. I think we both felt the need for a release of that pressure, I know I did, being all alone and not getting even a few minutes break each night. We started saying crazy things to each other like,

"Oh damn, looks like I'm going to have to get another window pane."

"Why do you need another windowpane?"

"Well, I threw my daughter through it last night and it shattered."

"Oh sorry, could you say that again? I couldn't hear you over putting my baby in the blender."

We would laugh so hard that we could barely breathe. The more absurd and off the charts demented, the funnier it was. I'm sure I just absolutely horrified some people but please don't take it wrong! The reason it was so funny is because we would never harm our children. The reason it worked so well is because in the midst of feeling incredibly tense and exhausted our laughter broke up everything and brought us joy. We never meant anything harmful and we knew that we trusted each other and ourselves enough to joke about the high intensity pressure that being a parent can create.

I remember sharing the aspects of our game with a man I was dating, he was totally disgusted. He is a *very* single man, with no children, never been married, lives his life just the way he wants to live it. He does whatever he wants to when he wants to do it and has no idea what it takes to be a parent. He is a children's book author and is incredibly romantic in theory so he was appalled when I told him what we would joke about sometimes. A few months later he and I and my daughter went on a long car trip to Canada. It had been a good trip but a trying one and on the way home my daughter was crying in the back for an extended amount of time, she was just tired of driving and was ready for some love. He looked at me and could see the tense grip I had on the steering wheel, and he said,

"Now, I get your game."

I started laughing really hard and so did he and the stress was relieved. It was nothing against Roxana as she was a wonderful baby and my friend absolutely adored her. It is not a personal affront to a particular child. Babies are babies, children are children and they are so incredibly beautiful and they go through so much. You just have to roll with it and it's not always easy!

Little Bits of
Encouragement

When you are overwhelmed and stressed... breathe, and allow the humor in life to flood your heart.

One thing I have to say about this is that *we never* spoke about anything in front of our girls. We never joked *with them* about it, never told them in a joking way what we were thinking of doing. This is for adults only, it is not for children to overhear and feel bad about themselves. It really has nothing to do with your kids, they are perfect in themselves. This is for adults who need a release, it is for parents who need more than anything, an opportunity to express their frustration in a way that isn't scary or guilt based.

Parents need to stop trying to act like we are tougher than nails! It is the type of person, the kind who denies their feelings and bottles up their idea of perfection that snaps and destroys their family in rage. Our little game may not work for everyone. We haven't played it in the longest time. I guess we don't need it anymore. The point is to realize, in whatever way works for you as a parent, that your feelings are totally valid and that you are not a bad person for *feeling* on the edge. The point is to *not go over* the edge. Do whatever you can to release that

pressure before it's too late. Also, if you have gone over the edge, there are many people out there to help. Get back on track, love your children and love yourself.

Child Abuse:

My theory on child abuse and how it is directly related to practicing extended diaper training begins with the reality that according to the American Academy of Pediatrics (AAP), "...more abuse occurs during toilet training than during any other developmental step."

Here are just a few gut wrenching cases that were reported in the Wichita Eagle (KS) in 2009.

- *Memphis, Tenn., police say a 2-year-old girl was beaten to death by her father over a potty training issue.*

- *Sacramento, Calif., a 27-year-old man was arraigned on murder charges for allegedly throwing his girlfriend's 4-year-old son against a wall after the boy urinated in his diaper in the night.*

- *Phoenix, Az., a husband and wife were accused of severely beating their 4-year-old daughter because she had not gone to the bathroom.*

- *Columbia, S.C., a father is in jail after being accused of kicking his 3-year-old daughter in the head and stomach, critically injuring her, over potty training issues.*

- *Summer 2008, a little girl was severely beaten for soiling her diapers. She was then stuffed in a pillow case and trash bags and placed in the attic. A medical examiner said the girl was likely still alive and suffocated over the course of several hours.*

"Those frustrating times in a child's development can be triggers, and we need to really... be aware of that as a community," said Vicky Roper, director of Prevent Child Abuse Kansas at the Kansas Children's Service League.

According to child development expert, Dr. Linda Acredolo, "The age at which children become really verbal (around 24 months) is likely to be when they also are beginning to strongly assert their independence. As a result, delaying potty training until they can talk all too often ends up involving a huge battle of wills."

Parents are told in our society, that their child has no ability or capacity to know they have to eliminate until they are 2 years old. It is recommended that parents wait *until* a child vocalizes that they are ready for potty training. Let's take a look at this idea from the perspective of the parent and the child. For the parent that means a minimum of two solid years of dirty diapers all day and night. That is a lot of work not to mention stinky, messy, *expensive* work. I know I would be finished changing diapers if I had done it for two years straight.

At that age and older our children are so smart and active in many ways, they understand everything going on around them. The fact that a 4 year old is so capable can be extraordinarily frustrating for parents because they do not get why the child still has to crap in a diaper! I understand why a parent would fly off the handle if there was, yet another, accident with such an old child. I cannot even imagine Roxana wearing diapers at 2 ½ years old let alone 4! She is so smart it just wouldn't make sense. Parents deal with a physical and financial burden as well as a frustrating psychological dilemma.

Children have it even worse, they are the ones covered in their own feces. As much as I can understand a parent's irritation and feelings of being done with diapers, it is not the child's fault that they don't get it, it is the parents. We have to realize when babies are put into diapers they are *trained* that this is the acceptable place for bodily waste. Many children struggle when potty trained late because they are not just learning a new skill; they first have to *unlearn* a very deeply ingrained protocol. There are children who pick it up quickly when potty trained late but the majority struggle and have long lasting negative effects. Because they were improperly trained to dispose of feces and taught to ignore their bodily functions and instincts; many children have a very difficult time reconnecting with their bodies signals.

With older children the shame and guilt is greater. Their friends don't have problems, their parents are unhappy, they are experiencing personal failure and it devastates them. All of this fear, worry, and embarrassment create an even stronger inability to reconnect with their natural instincts. As doctor Acredolo pointed out, when children reach 2 years of age and older they are also discovering that they are individual units and it is very important to them to be independent. All of the changes, confusion and new rules come at a time when all the child wants to do is play and explore. Children at this age tend to ignore what their parents tell them and will stand up for their "rights" with much more conviction. Not only are they going through this new biological struggle they are also being asked to tap into a bodily sensation they have completely ignored their whole life. When we understand the gravity of what is happening within the child it makes sense why so many have such a hard time.

The disposable diaper reliance that has been created over the past 50 years is a detriment to the health and safety of our children. There are record numbers of kids wearing diapers into their 5th and 6th year for overnight accidents. A friend of mine shared with me that his daughter wore pull-ups until she was 7 years old! If babies are given the opportunity to connect with their bodies' functions and taught to use a potty instead of diapers for such an extended period, they will be much more in tune with their instincts. This vital awareness substantially lessens the time for accidents and embarrassment.

Caregivers will obviously have to change their patterns and behaviors. It is my hope that we learn to trust our babies and listen to them, by giving them the potty training opportunities they deserve in the beginning. Through education and support parents can be taught and trained to pay attention to their infants elimination needs and therefore accomplish potty training *by* 2 instead of 3 and up. It is my belief and hope that this practice will greatly reduce the amount of potty training related abuse cases.

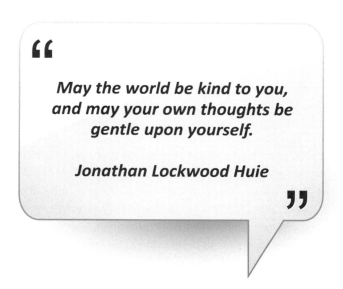

"

May the world be kind to you, and may your own thoughts be gentle upon yourself.

Jonathan Lockwood Huie

"

Child Molestation:

We, unfortunately, cannot come up with a solution to stop child molestation altogether as this tragic experience continues to devastate innocent life after innocent life.

I believe by fostering in our babies a strong sense of themselves, a clear understanding of their bodies and the functions of their genitals we can start our children off with a sturdy foundation. If an adult comes after a child with the intention of molestation they can easily overpower a child. Yet, a child who very clearly knows personal boundaries and is comfortable with their own genitalia has a far better chance of not believing what the attacker tells them and will immediately report any violations to their trusted adult.

Statistically, child molestation becomes ritualistic for the offender; these cases are typically the most devastating of experiences. If a child was raised from the very beginning with knowledge of his/her body then maybe the act would be brought out into the open after the first incident and not years later with undue torment. This way the molester could be dealt with before they made it a habit with one child or a series of others. The best way to fight situations like these is through awareness and through the empowerment of our children. This brings me to connect PTBT Method as a means of minimizing repeated child molestation.

If you think about a typical diaper trained American child, they are put in diapers at birth and they wear them 24 hours a day, except when in the bath. This consistent coverage lasts for two years at a minimum. On average American children are potty trained at 35 months for girls and 39 months for boys, this is the *oldest potty training age in history and throughout the world*.

Within diaper training the child is *taught*, even if indirectly, that his/her genital regions are hidden, dirty places that don't really belong to them. They are taught to ignore the sensations of poop and pee coming out of them, to not talk about what they feel "down there" and to go along with their life until someone notices they need changed. The only points during the day, besides bath, that the children may get a glimpse of their "privates" are during diaper changes. If children try to reach down and explore what is there they are often told not to, their little hands are moved away and they are given zero control or power over their own bodies. Instead, whoever is changing him/her has the power, this bigger person; whether mom, dad, teacher or caretaker, *they* are the ones with permission to touch and wipe up, powder and rub down his/her body.

The longer children stay in diapers the more access people have to their genitalia and the more *routine it becomes to have someone touching their genitals*. Parents, aunts, uncles, friends, babysitters, childcare workers, teachers, etc.; whoever happens to watch your child. A PTBT Method trained 4 year old may still require help to wipe his/her butt after a poop, but the person wiping is doing a very quick and non invasive act and the caretaker will not be hovering over him/her with the child's genitals completely exposed. The wiping up process for a potty trained child consists of one small area and not the entire region that pooping in a diaper requires. A child lying down while somebody else has the permission to touch them is *not* a position of power and strength and is *not* a position a child should become accustomed to.

Roxana has been wiping her own vagina for well over a year now but still does need help wiping after poop, although, she is *never* in a situation where she is lying down and someone else has control of her genitals. I fully believe that with her awareness and personal comfort with her body that if anyone were to try to molest her by touching her butt and/or vagina extensively or making her lay down in some position, she would know it was wrong. No matter what the person said to her, Roxana would intuitively and *logically* recognize the experience as *very different* from her *normal routine*. The molestation would be uncomfortable, hugely invasive and weird and she would tell me. Then I'd take that person for a long walk off a short pier, *if you know what I mean...*

Parents who actively tell their children that their private parts are just that, *private* and who take the time to verbally educate their children about what to do if someone tries to touch them are on the right track. However, this information can be very confusing for a child and definitively sends mixed messages while a child is still in diapers and is experiencing someone else constantly touching their genitalia. To tell a child they are in control of his/her genitals and then to show them the opposite can be very hard on them. It's important to minimize the extended ownership of privates by parents. Our children deserve to be able to know and understand their bodies, the earlier the better.

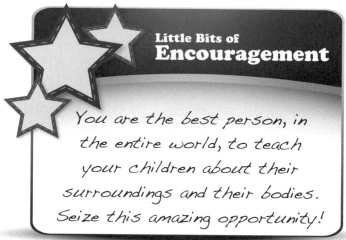

Little Bits of
Encouragement

You are the best person, in the entire world, to teach your children about their surroundings and their bodies. Seize this amazing opportunity!

I spoke with my daughter from birth about our vaginas' and butts and what comes out of them. She was fascinated by her own processing body. Now that she is a little older one of her favorite books is about the human body and its functions. She can see pictures of our digestive track and what happens to the food we eat. We also have an open door policy at home and often use the bathroom together.

There is zero shame in eliminating and in our genitals. When her father would spend time around the house she would see him pee and ask about his penis. She thought it was very curious and called it a "straight 'gina". We talked about how that was her daddy's penis, that was how he released pee and it was not for anyone else to touch, just like her own special vagina. Practical communication has been my motto when it comes to our bodies. In my mind there is no reason to skip any of these basic facts. Knowledge is power and tiny humans need all the power they can get!

Because Roxana spent most of her time wearing pants instead of diapers she was able to explore herself. I remember points when she was sitting on the carpet and asking me,

"Mom, can I put this toy in my 'gina?"

I answered back very simply, *"No sweetie, we don't put anything in our 'gina's, they are very sensitive and very special, we never put anything in our vagina's."*

"Ok, mom, can I put this spoon in my 'gina?"

And again I would explain! By allowing her the opportunity to touch herself and see what it feels like, to learn and know from her own hands that this area was hers and hers alone she has been greatly empowered.

Another key thing to think about is allowing our babies to experience how good it can feel to touch themselves. If a child has the opportunity to touch their genitals and they know that it feels pleasurable sometimes then they are *familiar* with those sensations, they are *familiar* with what is possible. Imagine a child who has never experienced this kind of sensation before and now they are 4 and they are molested by someone. The child may intuitively know it's wrong, they may be scared to death, and the molester may have threatened them or told them it was some kind of special game.

Yet, the child may have experienced for the first time in their lives a genital sensation that felt kind of good.

Do we realize how incredibly confusing and scary this can be? What does a tiny, innocent child do in such a situation? Being so afraid and feeling uncomfortable coupled with the little inkling of pleasure they may have felt? I'll tell you what they'll do; they'll be destroyed for the rest of their lives from this kind of trauma. I would much rather have my daughter know full well that she can make herself feel good, than have her find out in some horrifyingly confusing rape situation.

I believe by minimizing the time and the environments for children's genitalia to be exposed to various adults will help to decrease potential molestation. I believe by teaching our children healthy, positive lessons about their bodies through observation and communication this will greatly reduce the potential for a cycle of molestation to take root. The only thing we can do to truly protect our children is give them the tools to protect themselves. The best tool for children making their way through an overwhelming world is to learn to communicate their feelings and experiences. By empowering our little babies from the beginning of their lives, we are giving them a fighting chance.

Education:

I believe by practicing PTBT Method children have the potential to develop stronger mental capabilities and a deeper sense of intuition. By dealing with a child's basic needs in the beginning of their lives like proper diet, adequate sleep and healthy effective elimination cycles, this creates an enormous new world for them. Children who are potty trained early do not have to spend any time during their toddler days worrying about a possible accident or thinking about any bodily function issue, it comes naturally to them. Just like how toddlers play until they are hungry and then they eat, there is no fear or worry or stress. When a toddler is potty trained they do the same thing. They will dive into their imaginations without a second thought to their elimination needs or to an uncomfortable diaper dragging them down.

At 2 years old there is so much to learn for little people! Many are beginning to talk and express themselves in very funny ways. They are learning to be independent and beginning to understand they are separate from their parents. It is a time of defiance and personal space. This is a time that children need to be able to express themselves and explore, not be dealing with frustrating potty training issues. Trying to potty train a child starting at 2 or 3 is really the toughest time because he/she doesn't want to do what parents say anymore! Besides it gets in the way of all these new adventures that they are old enough to investigate! I am hugely thankful to see Roxana so engaged and to know that she's got nothing to worry about except what *"migration"* means, which she asked me the other day. Using the bathroom is as second nature to her as it is to adults.

Roxana was breastfed for 2 ½ years and I know that is a huge factor for brain development but I was not able to afford anything special for education. She didn't even have the luxury of having two parents catering to her educational needs. I did not use any learning videos or flashcards. Roxana is so smart because I feed her a healthy diet, because she gets exercise and adequate sleep, because I talk to her like she understands and communicate very clearly with her about everything and because she was given the opportunity to know her body, to trust her instincts, to develop a strong self esteem and understand her intuition. Many people would benefit with an introduction to our personal intuition. We do not spend time in our society cultivating, exploring or giving credit to the unknown, the intuition. Parents who raise their babies with the intention to learn this precious gift are opening up doors for their children that no one else bothers to open. The doors of each child's personal truth.

At 2 ½ Roxana knows the whole alphabet, all of the colors; she has an extensive vocabulary, counts to 20 in English and 10 in Spanish and can finish a 48 piece puzzle in less than fifteen minutes. She is hugely creative and imaginative in her play. In my observation, I see her deeply engrossed in all of her activities and then suddenly, she'll pop up and yell that she has to poop and will run to the bathroom. Once she's finished and washed up she's back at it. There are no limitations or fears and nothing is interfering with her growth and development.

Late potty training creates obstacles for a child's natural learning potential. By allowing our children to learn about their bodies and in effect control them at an earlier age we are opening up their minds to many more activities and ideas instead of bogging them down with basic physical functions. In this way and in my experience I have seen PTBT Method benefit my daughter from an educational perspective. I hope to hear some great stories from other parents who have witnessed similar growth patterns in their babies!

Your Own Incredible Journey...

Thank you so much for buying my book and taking the time to read about our wonderful adventure! I am so very excited about PTBT Method and feel honored to have had such a life changing experience with it. My love and Roxana's love for this practice is obvious and I aim to help instill this feeling in as many parents as possible!

Sustainability is a key word in our modern culture and I have found that practicing potty training with your baby offers a sense of sustainability in numerous ways. The beauty that you observe in your own personal growth as well as that of your child will astound you. The huge environmental impact that can actually be accomplished through one family's dedication to potty training is a force to seriously consider. The financial savings continue to come in long after your child is potty trained through the absence of diaper related physical and psychological issues.

It is my hope that by sharing our story, our trials, tribulations and the great successes, that parents feel a common bond and recognize their own desire for stronger connection. There couldn't be a better or more prudent time for this kind of change than right now. Our world is shifting in so many ways, people are grasping for deeper meaning in their lives and our environment is suffering exponentially, even worse than our pocketbooks are! There are a handful of books written on the subject by brilliant women. The wealth of knowledge and experience these women offer must not be overlooked by our culture. It is time to create a change together, by supporting each other in our efforts.

It is important to remember, while you begin your own journey, that our children are human after all and they aren't *always* consistent. Just like their other habits, interests and abilities, they are constantly changing and so will their communication about their bodily functions. Most importantly your children will learn to trust themselves. They will be able to recognize their own biological needs and will trust you and others to respond to them in a loving manner.

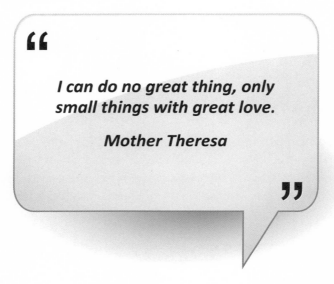

> " *I can do no great thing, only small things with great love.*
>
> *Mother Theresa* "

I send patience and courage to all caretakers as they see themselves through this. You will be amazed, you will no longer look at babies the same, your mind will be changed, and you will feel proud and happy. Your baby will be joyful and secure. You will think your infant pooping on the toilet like a regular person is the cutest thing you have ever seen; at that point you will know that your life has changed for the better!

I was just in the bathroom with Roxana, my just over 2 ½ year old daughter, getting ready for an afternoon nap. She brushed her teeth and while I was finishing up I told her to try to pee before her nap. She sat on her potty chair and gave it a go.

She said, "Mom, it's not coming out. "

I began making the pssst cue; she stared at me while I made the sound three times with a big breath in between each set. By the third she was peeing and sporting a huge smile with wide eyes as I haven't made the cue noise in quite some time.

I said, "Did your pee come out?"

"Yes, mom; Wow, it did!"

I said. "It's magic."

"Yeah, *magic*!" Roxana exclaimed while bounding up from her potty chair.

"Like when Pinocchio turns into a *real* boy!"

I laughed deeply, "Yep, honey. Just like that... *just like that*."

References

Websites:

www.pottytrainedbytwo.com
Angela Graham's website offering training, coaching, support, books, potty training gear and resource connections

www.thediaperfreebaby.com
Christine Gross-Loh's website featuring her book

www.wonderbabydesigns.com
Baby underwear

www.diaperfreebaby.org
Support Network

www.timl.com/ipt/
Laurie Boucke's website featuring her books and answers to common questions

www.pottywhisperer.com
An additional site from Laurie Boucke, a little more updated

www.attachmentparenting.org
Fantastic resource for a more gentle and connected approach to parenting

www.lalecheleague.org
Support system for breastfeeding

www.askdrsears.com
Offers parenting advice

www.mamatoto.org
Resource for baby carriers and slings

www.diaperware.com
Resource for all kinds of cloth diapers

www.babyworks.com
Family owned organic and Earth friendly store offering great products

www.drsonna.org
Dr. Linda Sonna's website, you can ask questions and get valuable feedback.

www.weebees.com
A resource for a list of websites that offer natural and organic baby care products.

www.pottytrainwithbabysigns.com
Website promoting sign language use for potty training and in general

www.fightingagainstthechildabuse.
blogspot.com/2009/07/risk-of-child-abuse-rises-in- potty.html
An informative anti-child abuse blog

aap.org/practicingsafety/module7.htm
American Academy of Pediatrics website

References

Books/Studies:

Bauer, Ingrid
Diaper Free! The Gentle Wisdom of Natural Infant Hygiene.
NY: Plume (Penguin), 2006

Boucke, Laurie
Infant Potty Training: A Gentle and Primeval Method Adapted to Modern Living. Lafayette, CO: White-Boucke Publishing, 2002

Boucke, Laurie
Infant Potty Training Basics: With or Without Diapers...the Natural Way
Lafayette, CO: White-Boucke Publishing, 2003

Gross-Loh, Christine
The Diaper Free Baby
New York: Regan Books, 2007

Sonna, Linda
Early Start Potty Training
New York: McGraw-Hill, 2005

Sears, William, and Martha Sears, Robert Sears, James Sears
The Baby Book: Everything You Need to Know About Your Baby from Birth to Age Two
Rev. ed. New York: Little, Brown, 2003

Morgan, Laurie Annis
The Power of Pleasurable Childbirth
Lincoln, NE: Writer's Club Press, 2003

Natec, Elimination Timing:
The Solution to the Dirty Diapers War
Kea'au, Hawaii, 1994

Schmitt, B.D.
Toilet Training Your Child: The Basics
Contemporary Pediatrics
2004; 21 (3): 120-122.

Bakker, Wilhelmina.
Research into the Influence of Potty-Training on Lower Urinary Tract Dysfunction. Antwerp, Belgium: University of Antwerp, 2002. (This doctoral thesis summarizes most of the important toilet-training research investigations.)

www.childdeathreview.org/reports/
FL_2007CADRrpt.pdf
Florida Child Abuse Death Review